Good and Bad Religion

Good and Bad Religion

Peter Vardy

scm press

© Peter Vardy 2010

Published in 2010 by SCM Press
Editorial office
13–17 Long Lane,
London, EC1A 9PN, UK

SCM Press is an imprint of Hymns Ancient and Modern Ltd
(a registered charity)
13A Hellesdon Park Road
Norwich, NR6 5DR
www.scm-canterburypress.co.uk

British Library Cataloguing in Publication data

A catalogue record for this book is available
from the British Library

978-0-334-04349-2

Originated by The Manila Typesetting Company
Printed in the UK by
CPI William Clowes Beccles NR34 7TL

Contents

To my wife, Charlotte,

without whom this book

would have been much

the poorer. With grateful thanks

Preface

The title of this book, *Good and Bad Religion,* may attract controversy. In practice most of us judge religion day by day. Politicians hail the positive influence it arguably has on education and community cohesion, and celebrity atheists attempt to demonstrate that religion is 'the root of all evil', tarring the moderate majority with the same brush as caricature fanatics. Most of us make smaller claims about the positive or negative effects of religious faith on a regular basis. Billions of people hold to the truth of their own religious perspective with passion and commitment, and sometimes fail to see anything good in other religions. Yet despite their prevalence, such judgements do not usually bear theoretical scrutiny and it can be dangerous to stand by them for long. People risk being labelled as cultural imperialists or simply fundamentalists when they stand by their own views and will not listen to those of others. Members of religions who stand up against 'bad religion' within their own traditions risk being ostracized and reviled.

This book is absolutely not about which religions are good and which religions are bad. It is rather an attempt to arrive at criteria by which some manifestations of religion (which may be found within any or all traditions) may be described in these terms. As such, this book continues a debate that has been going on at some level for millennia, yet which is bound to fail. My hope is that in failing it may serve to revive discussion of the central question, promote evaluation of the things people do in the name of faith and encourage action by motivating individuals and groups to stand out against aspects of their own religious

traditions that need to be challenged and condemned. Such discussions, evaluations and actions will never be easy but are an
essential requirement for those who aspire to lives of integrity
and truth, as do most religious people. Anything less will smack
of expediency and weakness – hardly virtues prized by religion.

Taking a stand is never easy – it is always more comfortable to
acquiesce and to accept the received wisdom of one's community.
What is easy and what is right are, however, rarely the same.
Too often religious people see things as divided between 'us' and
'them'. They argue that 'whoever is not with us is against us' and
that anybody who challenges things done in the name of faith is
an enemy of all faith. This is a human reaction, but poor logic.
Evil is usually found in the midst of good. It is within religious
traditions as well as outside them that 'bad religion' needs to be
challenged and rejected.

Religion has indeed been responsible for great suffering, persecution, wars, death and hatred. It has contributed to the suppression of learning and science and the denial of human fulfilment.
Murder, cruelty and some of the most horrific tortures have been
practised in the name of religion by people who would ordinarily
be mild and compassionate becoming raging fanatics, convinced
they are right, intent on asserting and enforcing the primacy of
their understanding of religious truth. However, religion at its
best has also inspired the greatest music, architecture, painting,
philosophy as well the heights of self-sacrifice, love and compassion. It has called saints and moral heroes, as well as ordinary
people living ordinary lives, to acts of moral heroism and great-
ness that can only inspire others. Some of the most awesome
human achievements in all fields have been directly related to
the religious imperative. Most people would accept these claims,
and yet herein lies the dilemma and the theme of this book. Once
one says 'religion at its best', a contrast is being drawn between
some forms of religion and others – the others representing religion at its worst or, perhaps, religion at a mediocre stage where
it has degenerated into a form a social convention devoid of passion or real content. So a distinction needs to be made between
'good' and 'bad' religion.

This seems so simple and so obvious a claim, but it is fraught with controversy and difficulty. Many religious people would not accept any external means of validating their claims. Religion, for its many adherents, often includes the acceptance of a supreme deity and literal account of God's will, and should not, indeed cannot be subject to any external test. To judge God, God's words or even the actions of God's faithful followers by any human standard would be to suggest that God is not supreme or the religion not a proper account of the divine will. Alternative positions, it may be argued, are simply heresy. This book will argue that this is an unacceptable approach – there is too much bad religion around, and bad religion is plain dangerous. Further, a general feature of belonging to a religion is the need for conformity and loyalty, which can bind a community into a whole greater than the sum of its parts, but also discourage critical thought and stifle debate within religious traditions. Submitting to proper authority can easily be extended into failing to question the status quo and fearing to stand out against abuse of authority. This book will argue that conformity is misplaced if it results in a refusal to engage with practices that should be condemned. To refuse to criticize evil in the name of loyalty is not a virtue – it is to be complicit in the evil, even if the evil is being carried out in the name of the religion to which one belongs.

In *The Chamber of Secrets*, the second of the Harry Potter books, Neville Longbottom stands against his friends Ron, Hermione and Harry because he believes that what they are doing is wrong. He appeals to a higher standard than loyalty or friendship and is willing to act on this. At the end of the film the headmaster of Hogwarts School says to the assembled students, when talking about Neville: 'It takes great courage to stand against your enemies, but even more to stand against your friends.' Thomas Jefferson, in *Notes on the State of Virginia*, said:

Millions of innocent men, women, and children, since the introduction of Christianity, have been burned, tortured, fined, imprisoned; yet we have not advanced one inch towards uniformity. What has been the effect of coercion? To make one half of the world fools, and the other half hypocrites . . .

The same may equally be said of other world religions. Of course the burning, torture, exclusion and other sanctions sometimes applied by religion have been wrong, but where were the voices that stood against this oppression? Where were those who were willing, from within a religion, to stand against their own supposed brothers and sisters of faith and to condemn them?

To anyone who considers the effects that bad religion can have on individuals, communities and the world, it must be clear that the consequences of failing to challenge bad religion are simply too grave for this to be a permissible way forward. Many will immediately think in terms of acts of terrorism, which have dominated news programmes and government agendas around the world in recent years. Terrorist acts may indeed be driven by bad religion, but the *effects* of bad religion are far deeper, more common and more prevalent than these well-publicized examples. They are felt in every world religion. They produce injustice, oppression and discrimination, and destroy many more lives and stand in the way of more human achievements than terrorism ever could.

There is, then, a common responsibility to stand up against bad religion, even when doing so is difficult or personally costly. This responsibility extends to members of all religious traditions and demands a willingness to stand up against bad religion within their own tradition as well as to criticize it in other traditions. This means accepting that there is a meaningful distinction between 'good religion' and 'bad religion', and providing clear, consistent criteria by which to make this distinction, criteria that to date have been elusive. This is the aim of this book. If it succeeds, making the distinction will be justified, and every religious tradition will be provided with some tools for engaging with the bad religion practised in its name. As I say, attempting to arrive at clear and precise criteria is bound to fail, yet the world's religions teach us that there are some things worth doing even without any prospect of success, and this book has been filed under 'too difficult' for too long. To say that precise criteria may not be possible is true, but this does not mean that some criteria cannot be found.

Peter Vardy
University of London
2010

PART ONE

The Challenge

I

Atheism

'Celebrity atheism' attacks a straw man

Richard Dawkins claims that religion is the 'root of all evil'; he is not short of material to cite in television series, books and articles that attempt to demonstrate the truth of this claim. Yet while religion has undoubtedly been responsible for great evil, it has surely been responsible for enormous good. Throughout human history the vast majority of human beings have been religious. The very word 'religion' has its origins in the Latin for 'to bind together', and it has long been the cord of ideas, beliefs and practices that holds communities and societies together. It could be argued that one might as well blame the atrocities of history on the fact that people have worked together as communities and societies as label religion 'the root of all evil'. Certainly if people had never co-operated there would never have been a despotic regime, a war, no unjust judgements could have been enforced and no large-scale oppression managed. However, if people had never co-operated we would probably still be living on roots and berries in caves and there would be little in the evolution of human beings for Dawkins to wonder at.

Religion is not a consistent, monolithic phenomenon, and it resists being treated as such in argument. Just as the conflict between 'science' and 'religion' has been shown to be more complex than the nineteenth-century cartoons of Darwin-apes bashing bishops suggested, the contemporary conflict between atheism and theism cannot for long sustain itself in its present, superficial form. Not all of those with religious faith accept the biblical account of creation literally; many accept the theories of the Big Bang and evolution through natural selection as perfectly compatible with their creed. Not all scientists dismiss faith as 'anti-intellectual', as Dawkins does, and there are many eminent representatives of different scientific fields who practise religion, whether as Christian, Jew, Hindu or Sikh. Following terrorist acts perpetrated in the name of religion, whether in Northern Ireland, on the commuter trains of European capitals, in Russia or the United States and the extensive media coverage of them, strident atheists have gained a new audience in blaming 'religion' for causing the suffering. Many of the 'religious' feel unjustly attacked but have retreated behind the shield of loyalty rather than enter the fray. The result has been that some atheists have become minor celebrities, scoring cheap points off an opponent who has, for the most part, been absent or not engaged. Atheism of a particularly superficial form – which might be called 'celebrity atheism' to distinguish it from the many other more subtle forms of rejecting belief that will be chronicled below – has become fashionable and is apparently on the ascendancy, at least in Europe. Yet despite this, religion as a whole is not in decline, though worryingly its most liberal manifestations are. Faced with repeated attempts to tar all those with faith with the same brush as caricature fanatics, many religious people have done the human thing, have felt that it is a matter of 'us' and 'them' and have become more entrenched in their beliefs, less accepting of constructive criticism and internal dialogue. It could even be said that this conflict with atheism risks turning religion into the caricature of religion the atheists reject.

At root this conflict between atheism and theism is superficial and betrays a lack of clear thought on both sides. Each position feels threatened by the other; each wants to maintain the falsity of the other's position and the rightness of its own. Atheists reject *all* religion, labelling it as primitive, damaging and something to be suppressed. Religious believers are driven to affirm religion *in general* in the face of these attacks. The virulence of atheist attacks on religion puts believers on the defensive and tricks them into defending a straw man (which sometimes seems more like a burning wicker-man!) rather than, as they should, taking issue with the premises of the attacks. Both approaches are mistaken.

The atheists are quite right that there is much wrong with religion and that it has been used in damaging ways down the centuries, but the religious believers are also right in affirming the importance of religion to the human psyche and the dangers and, indeed, impossibility of seeking to eliminate it. In seeking to describe religion as a consistent and monolithic opponent, atheists are not usually willing to discriminate between different forms of religion or to acknowledge the benefits and value of good religion. Perhaps the reverse is also true: religious people need to discriminate between different forms of atheism, to be willing to acknowledge that some forms have merit. In the end, what both sides need to do is recognize that there is both good and bad in religion. 'Bad religion' needs to be opposed both by atheists and by religious believers, but what is good needs to be supported and encouraged by both sides as well.

Many atheists will feel this last is a step too far, largely because the very word 'religion' has become anathema, but this prejudice must be tackled. Religion has become, with certain people, something to be opposed at all costs, with little attempt to understand the diversity of different religious perspectives. In short, there is a failure to distinguish 'good' from 'bad' religion.

Philip Pullman's books, though popular, have been widely criticized by many religious people, particularly in the United States, as condemning religion and promoting atheism. However, these books could be interpreted in terms of rejecting bad religion and searching for a way of understanding the world and of living that goes beyond the material and the materialistic. In his *His Dark Materials* trilogy, Pullman brings to life a complex, multi-dimensional world where good and bad are very much present and where religion (as identified with the power structures of the 'magisterium') is severely criticized, shown to be repressive and political. In the third volume, 'God' dies. Depicted as a decrepit and senile old man with a white beard, this God is shown to be false and irrelevant. Yet no serious religious believer considers God in such anthropomorphic terms. Either Pullman is, like other 'celebrity atheists', attacking and rejecting a straw man, in which case it is stupid for religious people to feel defensive and come to the aid of something most of them never believed in the first place, or Pullman could be making a more subtle point, namely that much of what is called religion really is not religion, or is bad religion at work; in which case all supporters of good religion should support him wholeheartedly. Perhaps Pullman's books do not challenge faith in the 'Holy Mystery' (as Karl Rahner put it) lying behind the complexity of the universe. Rather he condemns the simplification of awe and wonder at the created universe, with its complexity, purpose and order, into statements of belief in and caricature worship-actions of a man-shaped model of God. His rejection no more represents a rejection of the transcendent God of intelligent theism than does the condemnation of idol worship by Abraham or the prophet Muhammad.

Atheism can foster bad religion by forcing religious believers back into a laager of self-defensiveness in which they feel called on to defend their co-religionists out of loyalty in the face of atheistic attacks. When the atheist condemns religion, those who take religious belief seriously will often feel forced to defend religion, even though this would include many religious practices and beliefs they personally would normally reject. There is an old saying: 'The enemy of my enemy is my friend.' When atheists launch blanket condemnation of religion, co-religionists feel compelled to defend each other and put aside the fact that, under different circumstances, they would have little to do with each other. Religious people therefore often end up defending bad religion because atheists have launched blanket denunciation of all religion. Rather than doing this, supporters of good religion should be willing to accept that many of the more rational atheist critiques have force and merit and need to be taken seriously. They need to be willing to condemn the practice of bad religion just as strongly as the atheist. In this sense, good religion and atheism could be on the same side, standing against bad religion wherever it is found.

Many people today dislike complexity and have increasingly short attention spans. They want simple answers that can be conveyed in short sound bites that suit the media. No wonder Twitter has become such a phenomenon! However, short responses can easily be twisted by headline writers – most religious leaders are aware of this. If, therefore, a senior Catholic were to denounce Catholic practices (either today or in the past) that manifested bad religion in action, it would be all too easy for him or her to be quoted out of context and condemned by other Catholics for disloyalty on the basis of press reports. If a Sunni Muslim scholar were to question practices in Islam that were unfaithful to its high ideals, then many Muslims would be quick to attack him on the basis of what he would be reported to have said. If a devout Orthodox Jew challenged present Orthodox political approaches in Israel, many from his or her own community would pronounce their strong disapproval of what journalists recorded as said. People generally like simplistic answers; they prefer black and white to shades of grey. Nevertheless, this book will argue that this is no longer defensible, acceptable or permissible. People, whether religious or non-religious, need to engage once more with complexity, to struggle to find out what is true and right rather than settle for what is simple, easy, too often misleading and wrong.

Atheism is as complex as religion

There has been a long history of atheism – those who have rejected belief in God, gods or any sort of transcendent order. Atheism has many different faces and many atheists reject not so much God as the claimed manifestations of God provided by many religious groups. In other words, atheism over the centuries has generally been a reaction against bad religion. When religious believers fail to recognize the debased religious claims made by some of their members, and when they fail to take a stand against these claims and their associated practices, they provide good grounds for atheists and those who reject religion in its entirety. Failure to distinguish good from bad religion contributes to the rejection of all religion.

Many consider that atheism is a contemporary phenomenon, but this is far from the case. The rejection of the god(s) dates from at least the sixth to fifth centuries BCE. In the East the religions of Buddhism, Jainism and some varieties of Hinduism (the Samkhya and the early Mimamsa schools) have been called atheist; however, none of these religions deny the existence of the gods or spiritual beings, they just reject their worship as a necessary part of salvation. The teachings of Siddhartha Gautama, Parshva, Mahavira, of Ishvara Krishna and Jaimini all accept the reality of supernatural beings and forces such as *Karma*, but their rejection of religious practices in their time led to their being called atheists.

The most explicitly atheist of ancient eastern traditions was the Carvaka school of philosophy, which developed in the second and first centuries BCE. It had roots in much earlier teaching, such as that of Ajita Kesakambalin, who was quoted in Pali scriptures by the Buddhists with whom he was debating, teaching that 'with the break-up of the body, the wise and the foolish alike are annihilated, destroyed. They do not exist after death.' This was disturbing even to Buddhists, who believed in the transmigration of souls and the ongoing cycle of *karma*, which evened out perceived injustices, ensuring that good is rewarded and evil punished in the end.

In Ancient Greece, belief in 'the gods' was used as a tool to foster political loyalty. Rulers were given authority by claiming 'endorsement' from the gods, in legend or in terms of signs – personal strength, wealth or fortune in battle. In ancient times a natural disaster could unseat a ruler, whose main claim to power was the ability to ensure the safety of his or her subjects. People would say that the gods had deserted and were punishing the ruler. Rejection of the gods was, therefore, tantamount to the rejection of political authority and hierarchy. This is going to be an important feature of the debate about good and bad religion as it is all too common for religion to be taken over for political ends. This is so widespread and so prevalent throughout history – and still today – that it should be a source of complete surprise that its effects are so commonly ignored. Bad religion is often religion motivated by non-religious factors, and the search for power often lies behind the manifestation of bad religion.

As early as the fourth century BCE Euhemerus published his view that religions were used to support the continuation of earlier political structures, though he accepted the existence of primordial gods. He was later criticized for having 'spread atheism over the whole inhabited earth by obliterating the gods'. As the later poet Al-Ma'arri wrote, 'So, too, the creeds of man: the one prevails until the other comes; and this one fails when that one triumphs; ay, the lonesome world will always want the latest fairy tales.'[1] His work could also be seen to have prefigured the observation of Marx that 'religion is the opium of the people' – used by rulers to keep people under control and loyal to traditional structures. Marx was rejecting religion as a political tool of oppression by the powerful against the weak. In other words, he was rejecting bad religion.

Socrates famously rejected the gods accepted by the state and was charged with being *atheios*. But he did not reject the existence of all gods or supernatural forces or levels of being – just the particular Athenian pantheon, which he considered nonsense. He stood against bad religion and its manifestation and refused to participate in what he saw as a dangerous fiction. Socrates, like his pupil Plato and Plato's pupil Aristotle, occasionally referred to supernatural realities – daemons, the possibility of reincarnation, the world of the forms and *eudaemonia*. Socrates and others, such as Diagoras of Melos, discouraged people from accepting and subscribing to the state religion. As a result they were seen as a real threat and dealt with severely. Diagoras was forced into exile after being tried for impiety, because he rejected what he saw as the bad religion accepted by the Athenian state, and Socrates was given the choice between exile and suicide.

Other Greek philosophers, such as Democritus, Leucippus and Anaxagoras, sought to understand reality through physical observation rather than metaphysical speculation. For suggesting that the development of the world might be explained in terms

---

1 See://www.humanisticstexts.org/al_ma'arri.htm.

of atoms moving in infinite space, or that the sun is a fiery mass, these early scientists were denounced as atheists because they did not accept literally the conventional, traditional myths. Epicurus similarly argued that the universe could be explained without need for a God hypothesis, a point that has been repeated many times in modern times, perhaps most recently by Richard Dawkins. In his book *On the Gods*, Theodorus of Cyrene perhaps went furthest in straightforwardly denying that gods exist.

In the sixth century BCE Xenophanes said that if cows and horses had hands, 'then horses would draw the forms of gods like horses, and cows like cows'. He made the point (later and most famously made by Ludwig Feuerbach) that people tend to project God in their own image, to create a God that fulfils their needs and wants. This implied that human beings created God rather than God human beings. In the following century the Sophist Prodicus of Ceos wrote that 'it was the things which were serviceable to human life that had been regarded as gods'. Epicureans such as Lucretius, in *On the Nature of Things* (first century BCE), went a step further, arguing that belief in God could be destructive and limiting. In his view, there was no need to be afraid of divine wrath or worry about an afterlife, as the gods would be supremely uninterested in human affairs. Without this fear human beings could attain perfect peace of mind. Different philosophers sought truth, and where religion was seen to stand against truth they were willing to stake their lives on rejecting what they saw as misguided and erroneous.

Atheism continued throughout the period of the Roman Empire. Early Christians were described as atheists because they refused to take part in the state religion. They rejected and stood against what they rightly saw as debased or bad religion and were thus seen to threaten the state. Greek movements such as Epicureanism continued and were also branded as atheist because they did not accept the gods of the Roman pantheon. Once Christians came to power, they explicitly condemned and persecuted any who opposed them, and the reactions of many of the early Church Fathers to alternative views on, for instance, the nature of Jesus, Mary and God were often extreme. Those who dissented from Christian beliefs were often branded as atheists. With the collapse of the Roman Empire the development of the history of atheism shifted east to what became the Islamic centres of learning. The Prophet Muhammad himself was accused of impiety and atheism for rejecting the polytheistic religion of Mecca. The Prophet rejected the debased religion practised by the tribes of the Arabian Peninsula and sought to influence people towards what was good and seen as right – the growth of Islam was directly related to its being seen as positive and good in contrast to what went before.

The founder of Islam, therefore, clearly stood against bad religion, as did Abraham when he rejected the polytheism of the city of Ur in which he grew up. Abraham stood, according to the Qur'an, against primitive and debased forms of religion and sought to overthrow the idols worshipped, in their different forms, by almost everyone in his city. The result was his being condemned to death and having to flee because he dared to challenge the orthodoxy of his time. Abraham is regarded by Islam as the first Muslim, the first to submit to obedience to one God.

However, once Islam became established, then early Islamic scholars accused many others of atheism for rejecting what they saw as orthodoxy. Religious people and atheists have been united down the centuries in rejecting bad religion, although they often lacked clear criteria for deciding what was good and what was bad. Ibn Rawandi, from what is now Afghanistan, rejected any religious claim that was not within the bounds of reason, a move that prefigured the argument of Immanuel Kant by nearly a millennium. He was essentially an Aristotelian philosopher, believing that the truth should be uncovered through observation and reason and that all revealed religious truth and prophecy should be rejected if it did not conform to what could be checked. He dismissed the possibility of miracles and that any particular places or rituals could have religious significance. Abu-Bakr Al-Razi was a brilliant doctor who was also a more general scientist and a philosopher. He had read the works of Greek scholars and accepted the theories of Democritus, who saw that the existence of the universe could be explained in terms of atoms in infinite space without the need for a creator or sustainer God. He agreed with Euhemerus that religion was used as a tool by political leaders, and rejected Islam on the same grounds as Ibn Rawandi, arguing that all claims of revealed knowledge, miracles, prophecy and the power of ritual or pilgrimage were irrational and false.

The great poet Al-Ma'arri also denounced all superstition and dogmatism in religion, arguing that Islam had no greater claim to truth than any other religious tradition. A sceptic and a pessimist, he held surprisingly modern views, being a committed vegetarian and arguing in favour of birth control. Like Al-Rawandi and Al-Razi, Al-Ma'arri dismissed the plausibility of prophecy and observed that religions are all used by the powerful to control the weak. He wrote:

> Do not suppose the statements of the prophets to be true; they are all fabrications. Men lived comfortably till they came and spoiled life. The 'sacred books' are only such a set of idle tales as any age could have and indeed did actually produce.[2]

and

> They all err – Moslems, Christians, Jews, and Magians (Zoroastrians).
> Two make Humanity's universal sect:
> One man intelligent without religion,
> And, one religious without intellect.[3]

His point, that religions are generally destructive and the cause of great social conflict and personal unhappiness, has been taken up by many since. Again this deals in terms of generalizations as if religion is a single phenomenon and as if the choice lies between either a positive or a negative attitude to religion, whereas the issue is far more complex: there are many different types of religion, some of which need to be resisted and others endorsed.

---

2 See http://humanisticstexts.org/al_ma'arri.htm.
3 See http://centerforinquiry.net/isis/islamic_viewpoints/al_maarri/.

Freud noted the destructive effect of religious fear on the human psyche. He pointed out the damaging effect of religion and had a negative attitude to almost all of religion's manifestations. He parted company with his one-time friend, Jung, who took precisely the opposite view and held that in the case of nearly every one of his patients in the middle of their lives, their psychological problems stemmed from a failure to come to terms with the spiritual side of their nature. Both Freud and Jung again saw religion in monolithic terms – they failed to differentiate between good and bad religion and, by so doing, encouraged a simplistic attitude that was either in favour of or against religion, rather than one that differentiated between religion that was positive and religion that was negative.

Much atheism actually fosters bad religion

As can be seen above, atheism frequently arises as a reaction against bad religion and against the inadequacy of prevailing religious ideas. Most atheists hold that religion is a single phenomenon, to be rejected in its entirety rather than in some of its parts. It is precisely the simplistic notion that religion is a single phenomenon that this book aims to rebut. Because of this, it will criticize many, though not all, forms of atheism, alongside what best represents what they oppose in religion – those who deny that a religious believer should be able to think critically, both privately and publically, about their beliefs and all things done in the name of their faith without necessarily being disloyal and forfeiting membership of their religion. Creating out of the complex realities of religion a consistent and monolithic phenomenon is a work of imagination that may make the tasks of either rejecting it or holding it together much easier, but is a betrayal of the truth that most atheists claim to prize and most religious authorities to possess. Further, it leads to a mass failure to engage with how and why some manifestations of religion are bad; how and why they must be rejected without discarding much of what is good and useful and at the ground of many people's being.

It may be that in today's world there is a more important distinction than that between atheist and theist, namely that between those who pursue bad religion and those who stand for the truth and what is right, whether it be within or without a religious framework.

Both atheists and supporters of 'good religion' need to be on the same side in resisting 'bad religion'. One obvious way to make this distinction is to determine where truth lies, and it is to the issue of truth that we will first turn.

2

Truth

Truth is fundamental to religious faith. Religious people hold common beliefs in certain truths. A book that discusses 'bad religion' might therefore start by suggesting that some religious beliefs are misplaced or even false. There will be central truth claims or smaller issues of interpretation within any religious tradition, but once some truth claims are called into doubt this may raise further questions about the validity of the whole religious tradition.

Truth, evidence and value

A suggestion that a religion's belief in a particular truth is misplaced is likely to be based on at least one of two basic arguments. Either the belief is insufficiently supported by evidence and/or the belief does not fit with accepted or acceptable values.

The philosopher W. K. Clifford once remarked that 'it is always altogether wrong to believe something without sufficient evidence.'[1] From Clifford's perspective the only admissible evidence would be either inductive or deductive argument, that is either empirical evidence such as that used to support scientific truths, or logical evidence such as that used to support mathematical truths. It is clear that belief in religious truths rarely has such evidentiary support. The major arguments for God's existence have attempted to provide inductive (cosmological,

---

1 W. K. Clifford, 1877, 'The Ethics of Belief', in *The Ethics of Belief and Other Essays*, London: Prometheus Books, 1999, p. 271.

design, moral and religious experience arguments) and deductive (ontological arguments) evidence for the most basic religious belief, that a creator God exists, yet despite millennia of refinement within a number of different religious and scholarly traditions they are far from conclusive. Arguments from religious experience and from morality provide at best a reason to postulate God's existence. They cannot prove anything to a neutral observer and suggest, at most, that the existence of God might be a plausible or probable explanation for common phenomena.

The lack of inductive or deductive evidence in support of even the most basic religious beliefs would make being a theist, let alone anyone subscribing to the detail of any particular religious tradition, *wrong* for philosophers like Clifford. Many atheists reject religion because it promotes belief in truths that cannot be established. For this reason Dawkins has claimed that religion is 'anti-intellectual'; it fosters habits of thought that erode the mind's ability to search after and know what is really true. He has also described faith as a 'virus' that attacks the young and causes them to grow up thinking differently and less rigorously; effectively, to become defenceless sheep.

For those who accept the claim that any truth must be supported by either inductive or deductive evidence, belief in religious truths is arguably morally wrong in the way that taking mind-altering drugs recreationally is morally wrong. Any reasonable person knows that by taking these drugs they may be giving up their power of rationality, perhaps permanently, and that their action in taking them may influence others to do the same. No matter what apparent personal gain there may be in mental obliteration, it can never be acceptable. As John Stuart Mill said, 'I would rather be a human being dissatisfied than a pig satisfied';[2] human rationality is such a wonder that it should never be given up in the search for personal happiness or security, nor should one ever suggest otherwise to the impressionable, either in words or through one's example. Ludwig

---

2 John Stuart Mill, 1863, *Utilitarianism*, at http://www.sacred-texts.com/phi/mill/util.txt.

Feuerbach suggested that human beings subconsciously convince themselves of religious truths to satisfy their needs and desires, to make themselves happy. He went on to influence Marx, who equated religion with opium and suggested that it was not just being used by individuals seeking oblivion, thus causing harm to individuals, but was also being used by governments and those in positions of power who were 'pushing' religion as a means of social control. It is clear to see why atheists in this tradition see all religion as bad religion. Religions all promote belief in truths that cannot be supported by inductive or deductive evidence and, as such, could be seen to promote, individually and institutionally, behaviour that devalues or even destroys human reason and thus will prevent the fulfilment of human potential.

Yet in this argument it is clear that there are at least two assumptions that must be identified and evaluated.

The first assumption to consider is that the only types of evidence admissible to support any belief are inductive and deductive evidence. Arguments from religious experience and morality, along with cumulative arguments such as those suggested in recent years by the philosophers Richard Swinburne and Keith Ward, all indicate that God is a valid postulate. Can it be wrong to accept the best working hypothesis to explain the available evidence (for instance, the fine tuning of the universe) in the absence of evidence to the contrary? If this is wrong, much of the business of science would be undermined. Currently most scientists accept evolution and natural selection. Arch-Darwinians such as Dawkins suggest that the weight of evidence is so great as to allow scientists to talk in terms of truth and knowledge, to speak of the *laws* of evolution and natural selection rather than the *theories* of evolution and natural selection. Further, most scientists accept that the universe began with a Big Bang and that it is still expanding, and some have suggested that the weight of evidence is sufficient to talk about the Big Bang as a fact. Yet neither belief in evolution through natural selection nor in the Big Bang can be supported with conclusive inductive or deductive evidence. Scientists generally accept the *principle of falsification*, which holds that something can reasonably be believed unless evidence to the contrary is discovered to falsify such belief. At the present time evolution and the Big Bang theory seem the most likely hypotheses to explain facts as we know then, but there is always the possibility of the theories needing to be radically revised in the future. It is by theories being revised and shown to be mistaken that science advances. There are good arguments to suggest that the complexity and extreme improbability of the conditions necessary for the universe to form demand an intelligence. This hypothesis, it is claimed by some scientists, is the best explanation for the facts as we know them. What cannot be done is to suggest that such an hypothesis can be simply dismissed without argument.

There are those who have tried to claim that religious truths have been falsified, thus that those who still believe or promote belief in them are wrong, just as a scientist who hung on to a disproven theory would be. Yet in the 1960s the dominant theory was in a 'steady state' universe. Powerful voices argued that the weight of evidence falsified the theory that the universe had a beginning, and that those who argued such a position were simply wrong. It is just as difficult to falsify a belief conclusively as it is to verify it conclusively using inductive and deductive evidence. The philosopher John Wisdom used his famous 'Parable of the Invisible Gardener' to explore this point. Imagine that there is a garden and that two people walk past it day by day, never seeing anyone work in it. One might reasonably believe that there is a gardener who takes care of the garden, pointing to the apparent design, the presence of plants and trees, the wall and gate. The other might reasonably argue that there is no gardener, pointing to the presence of weeds, long grass and peeling paint. They cannot watch the garden 24/7 – even if they could, they could not rule out the existence of an invisible gardener – so neither belief is either verifiable or falsifiable. Similarly, one person might believe in God and another might not believe in God, but in the end neither belief is either verifiable or falsifiable.

Atheists in the tradition of Clifford, such as the philosopher A. J. Ayer, would argue that discussing beliefs that can be neither verified nor falsified is meaningless, nonsensical. However, few people would accept this. Every day we discuss many things that can neither be verified nor falsified. Love, beauty, right and wrong are just some of these things. Few people would accept that discussions about human feelings and relationships, art or morality are all meaningless nonsense. It seems that arguing that all beliefs must be supported by evidence, and holding such a narrow definition of evidence, leads to an impractical position at the very least. Keith Ward argues that 'ontological naturalism', basing one's world view on the belief that the material world is all there is, usually leads to conflating truth with what can be verified and, further, that the belief that material explanations can be comprehensive and can provide a full account of the nature of reality itself cannot be verified.[3] It therefore amounts to an unsupported faith claim. Furthermore, because the assumption behind ontological naturalism is so rarely pointed out, it has become orthodoxy, a position 'everybody' accepts, and questioning it has become unacceptable. Evidence against ontological naturalism is routinely dismissed or explained away without proper consideration; in short, the acceptance of ontological naturalism has become unfalsifiable and amounts to little more than a faith statement. Acceptance of assumptions that 'everybody' regards as obvious, and using the prevalence of one's belief to dismiss all opposition, often leads to bad science and bad philosophy. 'Everybody' once accepted that the earth was flat and that the execution of anyone who suggested otherwise was reasonable. It may therefore be concluded that by its own standards ontological naturalism could be judged meaningless nonsense; being an ontological naturalist may be illogical as well as impractical. This is not to say that ontological naturalism is necessarily false – just that it is a faith hypothesis that cannot be proved to be true.

Many of the world's religions have been influenced by the writings of classical Greek philosophers, including Plato and Aristotle. Plato saw this world as a shadow of metaphysical reality.

---

3 Keith Ward, *Pascal's Fire: Scientific Faith and Religious Understanding*, Oxford: Oneworld, 2006.

Famously, in *The Republic* he used the analogy of a cave to explore this. In the cave people are chained up facing the rock wall. Behind them their captors are carrying various objects around, and the shadows of these are cast by the light of the fire onto the walls. For the prisoners, who have been in the cave so long, reality is limited to those shadows. They are not able to experience objects in three dimensions or see them in full light. This is not to say that the objects *are* just shadows, just that the prisoners' limitations mean that the shadow is all they can know of the objects. For Plato, the philosopher should seek to escape limitations and discover metaphysical reality, howsoever possible and whatsoever it may cost. The analogy of the cave goes on to tell of the fate of the prisoner who escapes, sees the world outside as it really is and then returns to tell the other prisoners that their reality is just a prison. Of course, they band together to kill him for his pains. The analogy of the cave will be familiar to many religious people, not least because similar stories are contained within various holy texts. Prophets are rarely received well when they deliver revelations about the limitations of this world, its structures, beliefs and practices.

Aristotle saw the world rather differently. For Aristotle, this world is all we can know and therefore we should not waste time speculating about metaphysical truth beyond it, rather we should seek to understand as much as we can about what we can know and leave things at that. The philosopher, for Aristotle, must be a scientist, enquiring about all aspects of nature, pondering scientific findings to discover the laws that govern nature. For Plato, and even more for other classical thinkers such as Protagoras, 'man is the measure of all things'. Human experience and reason define the limits of knowledge and therefore reality; truth for us must be within the limits of that experience and reason.

Many of the world's religions have been influenced by both Plato and Aristotle. Aristotle's method has provided the basis for the philosophy of 'natural law', which has driven the pursuit of science and justice particularly within societies under the influence of Christianity and Islam. Scientists, including Charles

Darwin, were inspired to study nature and its governing laws by their belief that in so doing they would discover more of the glory of the creator God. Plato's belief in the limitations of this world has remained profoundly influential, however. While human beings must study and find out how the universe works using human experience and reason, this does not necessarily mean accepting that 'human beings can measure all things'. All flesh is grass; human beings are just one part of a much bigger reality and perhaps it is arrogant to believe that we could ever experience or understand all there is.

Perhaps the supreme act of rationality may be to accept the very limits of human reason and the fact that any human perspective on truth is just that. There may be 'something greater' (the transcendent, the divine or a perspective on life however this may be defined) that reason cannot fully capture. Religion claims insights into this 'something more' and does so because it claims truth. It claims access to something greater that is fundamental to a full understanding of reality. This 'something more' is at one level unknowable, but religion seeks to gesture towards it using analogy, metaphor, liturgy, poetry and even dance, though none of these can ever capture or fully define the object of religious reference.

It seems self-evident that religious truths are not like other truths; they are not verifiable or falsifiable as earthly truths are. Thus it is not possible either to disprove religious truths logically or to take the absence of normal evidence as evidence of absence of truth in religious claims. Religious claims, such as that God exists, that prayer is answered, that there is meaning to life or a life after death, obviously cannot be verified using empirical means. Therefore, as we have seen, thinkers such as Ayer argued that religion is nonsense. This is an understandable position but it rests on an assumption that may well be false. Einstein is quoted as saying that 'all that matters cannot be measured and not everything that can be measured matters'. Love, mysticism, beauty, the power of poetry and many other areas of life cannot be proved using rational categories. There are, of course, those who will reduce all such categories and will seek to explain love, for instance, entirely in evolutionary terms. Undoubtedly the developing discipline of evolutionary psychology can explain a great deal, just as science can explain a great deal, but there is a gap between saying this and holding that psychology and science can explain everything. Religion, at its best, should see no threat from science; it seeks to explain things science cannot address. If one asks, 'What is the material world?' one answer (given by Gerard W. Hughes) is that it is the world as accessible through science. In other words, the world that we know and experience every day, the material world, is the world to which science gives access. Yet that is not necessarily all that is.

This was essentially Immanuel Kant's point when he argued that definite knowledge is confined to the phenomenal world – the world as we experience it from our subjective human perspective. However, Kant insisted that the noumenal world, the world as it really is, objective truth, exists and is in every sense real – but it cannot be accessed by human beings because they can never escape their own limited perspective and must remain subjective observers. For Kant, the closest we can come to understanding truth is through aesthetic experience; we can make judgements about the way things really are but we can never claim definite knowledge of such. The aesthetic experience of great literature, poetry, art, music, drama, powerful liturgy or natural wonder can point us to truth beyond the limitations of human reason and science. If this is accepted, it is illegitimate to demand that scientific categories can be the only ones employed to measure religious and aesthetic truth claims.

Not everyone will accept this.

The second assumption that must be identified and evaluated is that human rationality and the discovery of truth through inductive and deductive enquiry are goods to be promoted, and that things that may hinder human rationality are evil. While most people reading this would probably agree with this assumption, it is important to identify it as such and to consider where it comes from. Plato, inspired by his teacher Socrates, argued that the ability to think for oneself and be rational is the highest human quality. Aristotle, inspired by Plato, maintained that developing wisdom and understanding of the natural world is natural to human beings and necessary to human fulfilment and flourishing. Immanuel Kant described human nature as driven by three appetites – the animal appetites, the emotions and reason – and, while he believed that all three appetites are good, they must be correctly ordered. Reason must be in control, keeping the emotions and baser appetites in check. The belief in independent, enquiring reason being humanity's defining and highest characteristic has a long history, yet it is a belief and it has just as little evidence in support of it as do most religious beliefs. Further, it may be from this belief about human nature that the general atheistic prejudice against qualities such as faith, obedience, simplicity, literalism and following one's emotions or feelings beyond reason may come. Therefore this prejudice (meaning pre-judgement), which leads many atheists to disparage religion, may be unreasonable and be effectively one world view shouting down another rather than arguing against it on proper grounds.

There is a tradition of turning to ancient Greece as the source of insights about humanity and of values, which are treated as if they are somehow timeless, not culturally or religiously specific, pure and somehow more true than insights about humanity or values taken from elsewhere. Jeremy Bentham, when attempting to devise a scientific system for determining right and wrong, turned to the Greeks to provide authority for his basic argument, that 'nature has placed mankind under two sovereign masters, the pursuit of pleasure and the avoidance of pain'.[4] Surely he could have cited many examples of people being hedonistic, but he could not prove that human beings are by nature pleasure-seekers, so he quoted a Greek philosopher to gloss over this problem and to give authority to his system. Alasdair MacIntyre, in his influential book *After Virtue*, did much the same thing.[5] After surveying the history of moral philosophy, he noted that no

4 Jeremy Bentham, 1789, *An Introduction to the Principles and Morals of Legislation*, Mineola, NY: Dover, 2007.
5 Alasdair McIntyre, *After Virtue: A Study in Moral Theory*, London: Duckworth, 1985.

one normative system had succeeded in providing useful moral guidance – so he turned back to the 'truths' of Greek philosophy to provide an authoritative basis for his new system of virtue ethics. In some ways it could be argued that some atheists are doing just this, objecting to theism on the grounds that it does not fit in with their belief in the primacy of human reason, a belief that lacks conclusive supporting evidence but may be lent authority by referring back to ancient Greece, or is held to seem reasonable because so many have already accepted it. Tertullian is quoted as asking 'What has Athens to do with Jerusalem?' or, to put it another way, 'What has reason to do with faith?' It is a reasonable question, and it is important to recognize that the acceptance of the primacy of reason is an assumption.

In a book about good and bad religion there is the assumption of values that transcend individual religions and indeed apply universally, by which religions may be judged. Determining these values is not easy, and it seems impossible to prove that the values by which religions will be judged are authoritative, let alone true. Perhaps it is for this reason, especially in a world that has been so dominated by moral and cultural relativism and in which people are reasonably sensitive about cultural imperialism, that books like this are rare. Further, as the next chapter suggests, accepting that there are transcendent and universal values by which religions can be judged is not something that will be easily acceptable to many religious people.

By their nature religions claim to possess truth and to offer the right way to live. Awkwardly, it often seems to follow that if any one religion's claims are 'true', then all the others' beliefs must be 'false' and the ways of living they promote 'wrong', except to the extent that they agree with the 'true' religion's claims. The claim of falsity would probably include non-religious systems that claim to possess the truth if it differs or perhaps even if it was revealed differently from that possessed by the 'true' religion. Thus it may often be the case that if someone believes in the truth of any one religion, they reject any philosophical system that claims to have objective standards by which to judge their religion, and thus would probably reject the conclusions drawn by anyone using the criteria suggested in this book.

Yet just because it often follows that acceptance of one religious faith will lead to rejection of other faiths and systems that propose alternative truths (or even alternative ways of uncovering the same truth), it does not mean that this is the way it should be. It may be possible that several religions and philosophical systems have uncovered the same essential truths in different ways. It is not possible to judge religious truths as true or false and religions as good or bad simply by appeal to objective, rational criteria.

So far in this chapter, two conclusions have been drawn:

1. Religious truths are not like other truths; they are not verifiable or falsifiable as earthly truths are. Therefore it is not possible either to disprove religious truths logically or take the absence of normal evidence as evidence of absence of truth in religious claims.
2. Rational categories are inadequate to understand or evaluate the depth and nature of religious belief. It is crude to judge religion as a whole, or any one tradition, as good or bad on the basis of questions raised concerning the rationality of its beliefs or practices, when the process of being religious seeks to offer insight into the limits of human reason and what may lie beyond.

Is it possible to approach truth in religion in a different way?

What is truth?

The problem of truth is simply stated: truth matters fundamentally to religion, but there seems no neutral way of determining whether or not a particular religion is true or false or even which religions have more truth than others. Religious believers tend to appeal to justification for the truth of their claims from within rather than outside their own framework. There seems to be no neutral place from which to seek to determine the truth of religion except a commonly agreed scientific basis and, as has been argued above, this is inadequate or unable to determine religious truth. Jews will claim that they are descended from Abraham, to whom God made promises to his innumerable descendants, but many secular scholars will question whether Abraham even existed, still less that the events recorded as relating to him ever actually happened. Muslims will claim the truth of the divine dictation of the Qur'an, but the reasons given to support this claim will not be accepted by Hindus or Sikhs. Christians will claim the truth of the incarnation, the doctrine of the Trinity and the resurrection of Jesus of Nazareth, but Jews and Muslims will not accept their claimed evidence. Theists will claim the truth of the existence of God, but their reasons for holding this view will not be acceptable to atheists or agnostics.

There are, however, alternative possibilities of understanding truth that depend on the nature of the truth claim being made. Put very simply, this is the philosophic difference between realism and anti-realism. Most religious believers are realists – this means that the truth claims they make are held to be true because they correspond to the state of affairs being described. For instance:

1. 'The Qur'an was dictated by Allah' is true because this actually happened.
2. 'Jesus died on the cross and rose on the third day' is true because this actually happened.
3. 'God made a covenant with Abraham promising land in Palestine to Abraham's descendants' is true because God did, indeed, make this covenant.
4. 'Human beings will be judged after death' is true because human beings will, indeed, survive death and be judged.
5. 'The way human beings behave in this life will have a direct effect on their *karma* and the form in which they are reincarnated' is true – and so on.

None of these can, of course, be proved to be true, although all will be passionately held to be true by those within particular religious groups. Truth on a realist view is based on correspondence between the religious claim made and the event or state of affairs described. Truth, on this basis, rests on religious statements successfully referring to the state of the affairs they describe. The problem with this approach – which is accepted by almost all religious believers – is that an immediate debate starts about which claims are true and which false. Religions seem to make competing claims that cannot be reconciled. Thus:

1. Either God is Trinitarian or God is not.
2. Either Muhammad was the final prophet sent by God or he was not.
3. Either human beings will survive death or they will not.
4. Either God exists or God does not.
5. Either human beings will be reincarnated or they will not.

Religious truth claims appear to compete, and contradictory claims cannot both be true. Alternative claims both maintain reference and both cannot be right. Sometimes this can be a matter of language. For instance, the Catholic and Anglican Churches attempted dialogue through ARCIC (the Anglican and Roman Catholic International Commission), a body that sought to reconcile Christian doctrines that seem to diverge. One way of trying to do this is to use new language. Thus Catholics held to a doctrine called transubstantiation which holds that, by a miracle, the bread and wine at Mass are literally transformed into the flesh and blood of Christ but, by another miracle, this is concealed from the worshipper so that they cannot recognize it. Anglicans rejected transubstantiation. The impasse seemed complete. However, by using different language (for instance, by saying that Christ is 'really present' in the Eucharist), the apparent dispute might be resolved. This approach, while sometimes helpful, cannot however resolve what appear to be such irreconcilable differences as those listed above.

There is, however, an alternative approach to truth that dissolves the problem. This is anti-realism, which argues that truth claims do not depend on correspondence and do not depend on successful reference. Truth, anti-realists hold, depends on what is agreed within a particular community. Truth rests on coherence not correspondence. On this basis truth depends on what is agreed within a given community and not on some independent standard. The tremendous advantage of this approach is that truth claims that appear to conflict, in fact do not.

1. Within Islam, the statement that Muhammad is God's final prophet is true; within Judaism it is not.
2. Within Judaism, the claim that Jesus was the incarnate Son of God is false, whereas within Christianity it is true.
3. Within Hinduism, reincarnation is true; within Islam it is false.

This seems counter-intuitive but in fact it is a highly persuasive position as truth rests on internal coherence within different communities. In the arena of morality, aesthetics and religion (and perhaps many other areas as well), truth is held to be relative to different communities. This approach denies any single understanding of truth. The enormous advantage is that the truth claims of different religions can all be held to be true since they all cohere or are accepted within the relevant forms of life (cultural milieux). All religions are thus true – by their own standards. None of them, however, make claim to reference – they are true stories in that the stories are held to be true by those who live by them. However, they are essentially no more than stories, albeit ones that provide meaning and hope for those who live by them.

The inadequacy of reducing this book to an analysis of truth claims

Persuasive though this anti-realist position may be to a Western academic audience, it does not capture the depth of commitment that religions across the world enshrine. People stake their lives on their religious beliefs. They maintain that these beliefs are true in an absolute, realist sense. They would utterly reject the idea that they are simply 'living a story'. Religion obtains its power because it is seeking to proclaim universal truth – and one reason for the decline of the power of religion in the West in recent years is that the idea of ultimate truth is widely rejected. Truth, today, at least in Europe, Australia and New Zealand (much less so in the United States), is seen as fundamentally relative. Postmodernism now dominates. There is no one thing that postmodernism is, but as Jean-François Lyotard says, it represents 'an incredulity towards meta-narratives' – in other words a rejection of any single story, any single way of making sense of reality.[6] Everything depends on perspectives, and different perspectives depend in turn on gender, sexuality, racial group and culture. When anti-realism and postmodernism come together, the idea of any single version of truth becomes an outmoded notion – one whose time has passed. Yet the realist claim that there is a single set of truth claims is precisely this supposedly outmoded notion that is at the core of religion. It is what gives religion its power and attraction – and also what makes it so dangerous.

If any particular version of a religion is held to be ultimately true, anyone who rejects this truth is in error and has no rights. The phrase 'error has no rights' has been used by the Catholic Church to justify the burning and torture of heretics. It was reaffirmed by Pope John XXIII in the introductory address to the Second Vatican Council. The Church, so the Pope said, does not set aside or weaken its opposition to error, but 'she prefers today to make use of the medicine of mercy, rather than the arms of severity'. She resists error 'by showing the validity of her teaching, rather than by issuing condemnations'.[7] This is a change in Catholic teaching and practice: previously, condemnations had been fierce and often vitriolic, with often devastating physical

---

6 Jean-François Lyotard, *The Postmodern Condition: A Report on Knowledge*, Minneapolis: University of Minnesota Press, 1984, p. xxiv.
7 John XXIII, 'Opening Speech to the Vatican II Council', 11 October 1962, at http://www.saint-mike.org/library/papal_library/johnxxiii/opening_speech_vaticanii.html.

consequences (the 'arms of severity' indeed). The change from coercion to persuasion in seeking to show the validity of Church teachings is significant – although, of course, there is still an insistence that the Catholic Church alone has the full truth and that error has no rights. If taken seriously, this is a claim that can be made by any religious group, and once accepted it can give rise to a great deal of bad religion. This is central to the argument in this book. Every religion can and does claim truth. Every religion appeals to its own criteria for truth, and these criteria are not generally accepted outside the religion concerned. Every religion is convinced that it alone is right or at the least that it alone has the fullness of truth. Almost every religion seeks to convert others to its truth and has been, at least in the past, willing to use any means to secure this conversion, including war, oppression, violence and torture. Many religions resist any challenge to their own truth claims.

This emphasis on the truth of religion is natural and understandable. It underpins all religious adherence and practice. No one, except for cynical reasons of self-interest, would commit to a religion they did not believe to be true. Once a particular religion is accepted it becomes necessary to instruct converts and young people into this truth. To confirm the validity of the framework adopted or the religious framework in which someone is educated is then vital to the religious enterprise. This will be done by creeds, catechisms, education, religious practices and other means, as well as by preaching 'the truth' in public worship to confirm the rightness of the particular religion's position and, perhaps, the falsity of others.

Groups often define themselves in terms of what they are not. Identity is often provided by characterizing an individual or group in contrast to others. Group definition often depends, therefore, on showing distinctive characteristics that others do not share. Jews do this in terms of diet, dress, circumcision and practices that 'set them apart' from the communities in which they live, such as treating Saturday as a holy day on which no work may be done. Muslims do this by praying five times a day, by treating Fridays as a holy day, by pilgrimages to Mecca and by fasting during Ramadan. Christians faced a problem in the early years of Christianity as Jesus was a Jew and most of his initial followers were Jews. The early Christian Church rejected the dietary rules of the Jewish community and opened their membership to non-Jews. What, then, was to demarcate Christians from the communities in which they lived? The answer evolved based on a strict sexual morality (which provided a marked contrast to that generally accepted in the Roman and Greek world), by faithfulness in marriage, by treating Sunday as a holy day and by taking part in the Eucharist, Mass or Lord's Supper. So religions separate themselves from others, and this separation is a major way of affirming their identity. The practices of separation are, of course, all seen as true and necessary expressions of the religion in question. While there may be many commonalities in ethics and morals across the religions of the world, in terms of practices and credal truth claims the divergences are considerable and are not reconcilable except at the most general level.

Those who seek a common core beneath all religions are forced to come up with claims of such vagueness and generality that few religious people would identify with them. It will not even do to claim that religion involves belief in God or gods, because many Buddhists precisely reject this. The issue of truth is, therefore, divisive and problematic in any discussion of religions in dialogue.

Truth claims are at the heart of all religious beliefs and practices, yet truth claims vary across religious traditions. Because truth matters so much and truth is universal, every religion seeks to assert that as it, alone, has the ultimate truth, its practices and beliefs should dominate across the world. The key move, which needs to be accepted today by those who wish to avoid bad religion, is that the spread of the truth of any religious view must happen by persuasion rather than coercion, and must be accompanied by openness to other perspectives. This, however, is problematic, as if any group is convinced that they alone have the complete truth, why should they be open to alternative perspectives that can only come from those who have a less perfect understanding of the truth? 'What has truth to learn from error?'

it will be asked. This is a central problem in any discussion of good and bad religion, as many will claim that since their religion has the truth, this must make it a good religion. This argument is no longer sustainable: it represents an assertion rather than an argument and, as has been made clear, an assertion that can be made by every religious group.

Theology is the exploration of the grammar of language about God. Religious language seeks to express divine mysteries in inadequate human words. It strives to express the inexpressible. However, language also defines orthodoxy and communities, as well as expressing the truth claims enshrined in these communities. Those in authority correct those who are followers. 'Say this, not that', the leaders will proclaim. 'This is true and that is false.' It is not that no other position could be right but that no other position may be held by those who are faithful.

The very word 'faithful' shows the issue. Faith, or fidelity, means accepting the truth claims of the religious group to which one belongs, and then living out the religious practices required by the group and established by tradition, as well as those seen by authority as enshrining the central claims of the group. Faith is encouraged not to question; and, indeed, questioning has often been portrayed as sinful or, in itself, wrong. True faith, it is held, is simple faith – the faith of a little child who does not question how or why but simply accepts. Jesus himself proclaimed that his followers should have faith 'as a little child'. This is an appealing notion, but in today's complex multi-cultural and multi-faith world it will not do. If everyone has faith 'as a little child', everyone will accept the faith claims of the religious group into which they have been 'formed' or educated, and any common ground will be impossible to achieve. The call to simple faith has too often been abused and misused. It has been employed to manipulate people, to discourage critical thinking and to ensure compliance. Good religion needs to be critical – not in a negative sense but to encourage people to think deeply and well, to be willing to question and challenge as well as to accept that faith, like love, may defy rational analysis.

Good religion requires priests or leaders who are well trained and intelligent, who lead their communities with compassion and understanding but who are also willing to wrestle with the complexity of truth claims in a modern world. Failure to do this and a refusal to engage in serious debate about the nature of religious truth claims is a feature of bad religion, and needs to be challenged and resisted wherever it is found. Yet while important to consider, analysing the nature of truth in religion is not going to provide conclusive guidance on how to differentiate between good and bad religion. There is no way of proving one religion to be true or more true than another, so truth is going to fail as a criterion.

The problem remains unresolved. How can one differentiate between good and bad religion if it is not possible to use rational argument to justify religious truth claims? The conclusion seems inevitable. If reason cannot differentiate between true and false religion, the very attempt to make this differentiation needs to be recognized as impossible. If this is accepted, then the position that also seems to follow is that good and bad religion cannot be differentiated. This would seem to follow logically, but it is precisely this simplistic conclusion that needs to be resisted. There may be other ways of separating good and bad religion that do not rely on an analysis of religious truth claims. This is not to say that truth does not matter, but that where truth cannot be independently determined, other criteria need to be applied. Establishing at least some of these criteria is the aim of this book.

3

The Euthyphro Dilemma

As we have seen, one of the biggest problems in trying to differentiate between 'good' and 'bad' religion is that most religions claim that the very standards of good and bad originate from their God; that they possess the truth about God's will and are justified in following it. If beliefs or practices seem irrational or are unacceptable to other groups, it must be because other groups are in error or in the dark about God's will. Religions can seem to be self-justifying. If one believes, then it is a good religion and all others are bad, but if one doesn't believe, then any claim that the religion is bad is made on the basis of incomplete understanding. Standards of truth and the right to judge may thus be exclusive, and any attempt to judge all religions according to universal criteria nonsensical.

Goodness is whatever God commands

Ethical monotheism argues that ethics rests on the commands of a single God. Ethical monotheism is thus a particular feature of the three great monotheist religions: Christianity, Islam and Judaism.[1] A more traditional way of describing ethical monotheism is as a 'divine command' theory of ethics. Ethics, on this understanding, is based on the commands of God. God is the creator and sustainer of the universe. God, therefore, has the

---

1 Christians, Jews and Muslims all believe in a single God – Christianity differs from Islam and Judaism in that it holds that God is a Trinity of three persons in one, but Christians insist that this in no way undermines the unity of the Trinity. It is *not* the case, as some critics sometimes maintain, that Christians believe in three gods – indeed, this is formally condemned as a heresy in Christianity.

absolute right to lay down the moral laws for God's creatures. Ethical monotheism is a realist theory of ethics because it holds that what is right and wrong corresponds to the command of God. Truth in morality is not a matter of opinion, it depends directly on God's will.

The claim that God lays down moral laws depends on revelation – in other words, on God's revealing what the moral laws are. Attitudes to revelation differ between and within the three monotheistic religions:

- Jews hold that they were given the definitive revelation of God in the Torah – the first five books of the Hebrew Scriptures which, according to the tradition, were written by Moses.[2] Of all the commands, the Ten Commandments were and are the most important, but the first five books of the Hebrew Scriptures give many other commands as well (for instance, not eating pork or the requirement that all male babies should be circumcised). However, there is also a strong tradition in Judaism that Jewish teachers or Rabbis need to reflect on the Law laid down by God and to interpret the Law based on the current situation in which the people of Israel live. These Rabbinic reflections, which have been written down and recorded, have almost as much influence as the original revelation given by God.
- Christians see the Hebrew Scriptures, the Old Testament, as being inspired by God and attach equal or greater importance to the New Testament – the four Gospel accounts of Jesus' life, the letters of Paul and others and the book of Revelation. However, Christians differ as to the main source of revelation. For Protestants, the Bible is central and thus the final arbiter of God's revelation to humanity.

---

2 The authorship of the first five books of the Old Testament by Moses was a belief also held by Christians. Today almost no Christian theologian would take this view – biblical scholarship has shown that there were many sources for these five books and that they were written and compiled over a long period of time.

Luther said that 'the plain word of Scripture' was the final authority in all matters of morality. We now know, however, that the synoptic Gospels – Matthew, Mark and Luke – are compilations, not written by a single person. Nevertheless, some Christians consider them to be inspired by God and therefore hold that they can accurately guide people in matters of morality. Catholics, however, see God revealing his will for human beings through the Church, which was founded by Jesus with St Peter as its first head. While the Bible is recognized as important (particularly after the Second Vatican Council in 1965), the Church is the final arbiter of God's revelation.

• For Muslims, the Holy Qur'an is the final and definitive revelation of God. The Holy Qur'an is held to have been dictated by the Angel Gabriel to the Prophet Muhammad and, therefore, to represent the final word of God on all aspects of a Muslim's life. The Qur'an contains teachings about every aspect of life, and obedience to the Qur'an is central for a devout Muslim. There is a limited amount of interpretation possible in the Qur'an as some passages are held to be 'abrogated' by others – in other words, some passages are given priority over others. However, in general, obedience to the exact words of the Qur'an is central. The status of the written word of the Qur'an as the divinely dictated word of God is higher for Muslims than in the case of the Jewish or Christian scriptures – both of which are seen as human records of divine revelation.

The first problem, therefore, with ethical monotheism lies in deciding which revelation of God to accept and how this revelation is to be interpreted. Interpretation is almost always required – for instance, the fifth commandment specifically states: 'Thou shalt not kill', but most Jews, Christians and Muslims consider that killing is permitted in various circumstances, including in warfare, in self-defence and, some hold, as punishment for murder or various other actions that are argued to be morally wrong (for instance, adultery in Islam in punishable by stoning to death). In the very next chapter of the book of Exodus, after the Ten Commandments are listed, four reasons are given for putting someone to death (when a man kills someone else; when someone strikes their father or mother; a kidnapper; or anyone who curses his father or mother – Exod. 21.14–17). Most people today do not take these commandments literally. Interpretation is therefore required to decide which commandments are or are not to be regarded as the direct revelation of God.

One of the major debates within the Anglican Church at the present time relates to homosexuality. Many evangelical Anglicans tend to condemn homosexuality and to maintain, for instance, that a practising homosexual or lesbian cannot be ordained as a priest or appointed to be a bishop. They base this on what they see as clear scriptural condemnation of homosexuality. Others, however, argue that the Bible condemns promiscuous homosexuality associated, for instance, with worship of other gods, and never considers the issue of a long-term, loving and committed homosexual relationship. They argue that biblical commands need to be understood in context and, out of context, are misleading. The difference between the two approaches highlights the difficulty of ethical monotheism and how much depends on interpretation.

God, so ethical monotheists hold, creates the universe and human beings and has the absolute right as the creator of everything that exists to lay down commands that his creatures should follow. God is free to decide how human beings should behave and has the absolute right to command as God freely wishes to do. As an example, in Genesis Chapter 2 God creates Adam and Eve and puts them in the Garden of Eden, saying that they may do as they wish provided they obey one simple command – the command not to eat of the fruit of the tree in the middle of the garden. Adam and Eve disobey, and some Christian theologians hold that sin, evil and death entered the world as a result. If anyone queries why God should have issued this command, the ethical monotheist's reply would be that God, as sovereign Lord of the universe, can do as God pleases and it only remains for human beings to obey.

This view was held, at least partly, by Thomas Aquinas, who argued that since God created and owns the whole of creation, it therefore follows that God could command anything he wished. Aquinas considered the example of Abraham and his wife Sarai who, in the Hebrew Scriptures, are recorded as journeying to Egypt. Sarai was very beautiful, and Abraham was concerned that the ruler of Egypt would wish to make love to his wife and would kill him to do so. Abraham therefore told Sarai to say that she was his sister, as then the Egyptian ruler could take her for his wife and make love to her without killing Abraham. Sarai did this, and she and Abraham were showered with gifts by the Pharaoh. Seemingly unfairly, since he did not know that Sarai was Abraham's wife, the ruler of Egypt was punished for doing this by God. However, according to Aquinas, the issue of fairness does not arise – God can do as he wishes and can punish and reward without any idea of fairness, but merely as God decides. Aquinas even argued that God could command a person to commit adultery, and it would not then be adultery since, as every human being is created and owned by God, God could dispose of his creation as he liked. Similarly, if God commanded theft, this would no longer be theft since everything in the universe is owned by God, the creator, and God can do what he likes with what God owns. Not everyone, however, accepts this view. Many philosophers, beginning long before Aquinas with Plato and up to, more recently, Bertrand Russell, rejected this view.

The great attraction of ethical monotheism is that it provides an absolute standard of what is right and wrong, good and bad that does not depend on human opinion or society but is laid down by God. Once a person has decided how to access the commands of God (which means deciding which religion to adopt and which understanding of this religion to accept), being good simply means obeying the commands of God. It is all very simple; but, of course, this is precisely the problem. In a multi-faith and multi-cultural world there is no agreement on which religion to accept, still less which interpretation to adopt. Indeed, the trend tends to be towards greater religious fragmentation, and this leads many people to reject any idea of God as a source of morality. Nietzsche took this position. When his character, Zarathustra, proclaimed 'God is dead' he was proclaiming not just the non-existence of God but the denial of any absolutes in morality. However, no religious person will side with Nietzsche. The problem is the increasing number of people across the world who look to religion as the ultimate arbiter of morality without engaging in further thought as to whether criteria exist for separating good from bad religion and, in particular, for evaluating the claims of those who argue for ethical monotheism and the claim that it is God's will alone that decides on morality and that there can be no appeal beyond this.

The Euthyphro dilemma

The debate about whether there can be criteria for differentiating between good and bad religion has a long history. Probably the most important argument to address this was put forward by Socrates and has become known as 'the Euthyphro dilemma'. Plato, Socrates' pupil, recounts the story of a dialogue between Socrates and a young man called Euthyphro whom he meets on the way to the city, where he intends to prosecute his father for actions that are abhorrent to the gods or, to put it another way, for impiety. Euthyphro's father had found two peasants quarrelling and had tied up the aggressor, meaning to report him to the authorities. However, he forgot, and the peasant died. His son considered that the father was guilty and should be prosecuted. The discussion comes round to the nature of the commands of the gods and whether these are good simply because the gods command them, or whether they are good because they are judged according to some independent standard. What is central for the whole discussion is to work out in what piety consists. This was important to Socrates. He was on trial in Athens on a charge of impiety, so he professes himself anxious to obtain a general definition of what piety is in order to use the definition in his defence.

Euthyphro starts by giving an example of impiety – namely the action of his father. This is rejected by Socrates as it is merely an example of impiety and not a general definition, which is what Socrates is seeking. Euthyphro's second attempt fulfils the demand of Socrates. He says that piety is what is pleasing to the gods. Socrates, while accepting that Euthyphro has fulfilled has request for a general definition, maintains that it is not adequate because the (Greek) gods often disagree and, therefore, there is no single view of what is commanded by the gods. Euthyphro replies that all the gods would agree that unjustified killing is wrong, but Socrates will not accept this – there will be arguments about what killing is justified and what is not; agreement will be impossible to find.

Euthyphro then provides his third definition – which is that piety consists in doing what *all* the gods love and avoiding those actions *all* the gods hate. Greeks, of course, in common with the Romans and the Norse people, believed in many different gods, and Euthyphro is effectively appealing to a consensus among the gods to determine what is good and what is bad, what piety is and what it is not. It is at this point that Socrates introduces what has become known as 'the Euthyphro dilemma', and this brings us to the heart of the issue. Is 'what is pleasing to the gods' (translated into modern religious terms this would be 'what is commanded by God') good simply because God wills it, or is there a standard of goodness independent of God against which God's commands can be regarded as good? Both of these alternatives have considerable problems:

1. If what God wants is good just because God wills it, we have what is effectively a 'divine command' theory of ethics. The modern term for this is ethical monotheism. God's will is the ultimate standard of right or wrong, and as God creates the universe so God has the ultimate right to decide on the standard of what is good and bad, right and wrong. Most Muslim commentators take this view and so do many Christians, including Abelard and Bonaventure. God's will is sovereign and is the sole standard for moral

behaviour. If this is accepted, good religion merely consists in obedience to God – whatever God wills is good and there is no way of questioning this, nor can there be any criterion for checking whether commands are really from a good God or not. Indeed, to call God good is a tautology, as whatever God wants is good, just because God wants it. 'God is good' becomes no more than saying 'God is God', since whatever God wants is good. In the Hebrew Scriptures there are what most would agree are abhorrent commands attributed to God, including that King Saul should slaughter all the women and children of a defeated enemy. When Saul did not do so, he was condemned and deposed as King by God's prophet since he had committed the ultimate sin – disobedience to God. Socrates rejects this option as an autocratic God would not be worthy of worship.

2. The alternative, which Socrates and Plato both argue for, is that 'the gods' are good when measured by a standard independent of them. They are rightly, therefore, praised as good when measured by this independent standard. The idea of an independent standard of goodness goes to the heart of Plato's philosophy. However, admitting that the gods or God are or is subject to judgement against an independent, transcendent and universal standard of goodness suggests that the gods or God is or are not omnipotent in the traditional sense, nor the creator of everything.

Socrates argues for the second of these alternatives. He draws a comparison with the use of the word 'carried'. We describe some object as being carried not because of something that is innate to the object itself but because it is being carried. For instance, a book, a glass of water or a pen may be described as being carried because someone or something is carrying it. 'Being carried' is not an innate property of a thing – it may be a correct description if and only if the item in question is correctly described as being carried. Similarly, Socrates argues, we call an action pious or good not because of some inherent state within the action but because it is regarded as pious or good when measured against some external standard. The gods, therefore, would like an action or consider it to be pious or good not because of the nature of the action in itself but because it is considered pious or good by reference to some independent standard.

Socrates contends, therefore, that the fact that 'all the gods' consider an action to be good or pious is because the action corresponds to some independent state of affairs against which the action can be measured. Euthyphro has nowhere to turn except to go back to his original claim that piety is simply what the gods love, and he rushes off to an important meeting. Socrates is left to defend himself against the accusation of impiety before all the free (male) citizens of Athens – an accusation of which he would be found guilty and which (combined with the associated charge of 'corrupting the young', because he taught young people to think for themselves) would lead to his being condemned to death.

Some Christians want to avoid the challenge of the Euthyphro dilemma by saying that God is the author of morality, but since God is an all-loving God, God would not command anything that went against the law of love. This is an attractive idea, but unfortunately it does not succeed as the problem moves from:

- Whether God is good because whatever God commands is good as God is the final arbiter of goodness *or* whether there is an independent standard of goodness against which God is judged as good, to
- Whether God is loving because whatever he commands is defined as loving as God is the final arbiter of love *or* whether there is an independent standard of love against which God is judged as love.

In other words, it is by no means clear what it means to say that God is loving. God is held, according to Christians, to have willed that God's Son, Jesus, should die on the cross. Jesus knew this to be the case and prayed to his father in the Garden of Gethsemane that this should not happen, but in the final analysis

Jesus was willing to accept God's will for him (expressed in Jesus' saying to his Father, 'Not what I will but what you will be done'). Many people might consider that a loving God would not will that his Son should suffer a hideous death on the cross, but this is held to be precisely a loving action by God. God cannot be judged in human terms and, therefore, what it means for God to be loving does not provide any clear criteria to overcome the challenge of the Euthyphro dilemma.

It is not enough simply to say that whatever the gods want is good just because the gods want it. This was formulated more clearly by Bertrand Russell when he argued that to make God the sole standard of what is good and bad gives no grounds for worshipping God. God cannot be worshipped because God is said to be good as this is simply a tautology: whatever God wants is good and therefore to say that God is good is really equivalent to saying that whatever God wants, God wants – it gets the debate no further forward. The only reason for worshipping God becomes that God is the ultimate power figure who will condemn and punish those who disobey and reward those who obey. Such a picture of God portrays God as rather like a super-Hitler figure in the sky and provides no moral reason for obeying or worshipping God. Those who obeyed Hitler were wrong to do so, even though obeying him brought considerable benefits and disobeying him brought severe penalties. It can never be right, so Russell argues, to obey an ultimate power figure just because of a fear of not doing so.

The whole idea of worshipping God depends on God being the sort of being who deserves to be worshipped and obeyed, and this, according to Socrates and Plato, must mean that there needs to be an independent standard against which God can be judged as being worthy of praise and worship.

This discussion has a profoundly modern ring to it and it is central to the aim of this book. If the only criterion for what is good is what God is (supposed) to have commanded, it is difficult to make a case for differentiating between good and bad religion. However, this brings the discussion to an important point. It is necessary to separate:

- those actions commanded by God from
- those actions supposed to be commanded by God.

These two are not the same. Gods down the ages have been supposed to have commanded terrible things, and many would agree (at least in retrospect) that these actions were not commanded by God at all. It is easy to list examples.

1. When the people of Israel came back from Egypt into the Promised Land, this land was already settled and peaceful. In a series of military campaigns the tribes of Israel destroyed the cities and killed the inhabitants at the command of God. The whole population of Jericho – men, women and children – were slaughtered at God's command.

2. Solomon is held up as one of the great judges of Israel appointed by God, yet he was vicious, vengeful, slept with large numbers of women, rejected his wife and then demanded her back again, and still God sided with him against those who opposed him, merely because he was a member of the house of Israel.

3. King Saul was deposed by the prophet Samuel because, after defeating his enemies, he had mercy on the women and children rather than killing them all as God commanded.

4. The tribe of Benjamin were slaughtered by the other Hebrew tribes because of an attempted act of homosexual rape and the rape and murder of a concubine of one of the other tribes. A few remaining males of the tribe of Benjamin remained and, in order to obtain the women necessary to rebuild the tribe, an armed raid is carried out on a neighbouring tribe to acquire the women necessary for breeding purposes.

5. The building of Jewish settlements on the West Bank in Palestine and the increasing annexation of parts of Jerusalem is agreed to be against international law. Israel occupied by armed force large areas that did not belong to it under international law and refuses even to negotiate about the return of these areas, partly for security reasons

THE EUTHYPHRO DILEMMA

but, more importantly, because they are held to have been promised to the people of Israel by God. Olive groves were destroyed (in spite of the fact that this is condemned in the Hebrew Scriptures), Palestinian houses bulldozed and civilians killed (for instance in the 2008 attacks on the Gaza Strip by Israeli forces).

The record of Christianity is full of vicious, cruel and inhuman actions attributed to the will of God. For instance:

1. The Christian Church campaigned against the Cathars in France in a crusade that resulted in the death of tens of thousands of people, many of whom lived simple lives seeking to be obedient to what they saw as the commands of God. Yet because their doctrines were at variance with the Church they were condemned. The Cathars rejected the pomp and wealth of the Church and called people back to the example of Jesus of Nazareth, but their understanding of God and God's relationship to the world differed from that of the institutional Church – so they were condemned.

2. Tens of thousands of witches were burnt by Christians who believed they were doing the right thing. These women may have been 'different', either physically or in personality, or they may have seemed to pose a threat to local church authority, for instance by challenging priests' teachings in ways difficult to answer either in words or actions, or by offering their services as healers or teachers when the local abbey saw itself as having a monopoly over healthcare or education.

3. The Christian Church forced Jews, in many parts of Europe, to wear a yellow star (long before the Nazis made use of the same symbol), forbade them to engage in normal activities, often stole their goods and branded them 'killers of Christ' because of a dubious interpretation of a passage in John's Gospel.

4. Protestant Christians sought to return to the word of God, which they held to be found in the Bible, and challenged

45

the authority of the Church in Rome. Thousands were burnt as heretics, and wars between Christians, supposedly fought in God's name, were common.

5. The institution of slavery, by which hundreds of thousands of black people were transported to the plantations of America in the most appalling conditions (in which most of them died), was not condemned by the mainstream Churches until the end of the nineteenth century.

6. The slaughter of the Jews before and during the Second World War was known about by many Christians (including Church leaders), but they chose to remain silent.

7. The practice of apartheid in South Africa was seen as commanded by God by some Christians and Christian Churches in South Africa.

8. The invasion of Iraq (described by President George W. Bush as a new crusade) was seen by both Bush and by the British Prime Minister, Tony Blair, as linked to their religious duty, but led to the death of hundreds of thousands of Iraqis.

In Islam, religion has been used as a pretext or at the least as an umbrella for terrible deeds, including:

1. The organization of the slave trade in Africa by Muslim traders, who were often the suppliers of slaves to the ships involved in the 'middle passage' from Africa to the plantations.

2. The rape and murder of tens of thousands of men, women and children who were Christians or Animists, in Darfur by Muslim forces that saw themselves as obedient to God.

3. The attacks on the 'Twin Towers' on 9/11 and on the London Underground on 7/7 by dedicated Muslim extremists who saw themselves engaged in a 'holy war'.

4. Attacks on Christian Churches by Muslim groups and the killing of Christian priests (for instance in Nigeria) are rarely condemned in forthright terms. Christians are not allowed to speak about their religion in Muslim countries,

and any Muslim who converts to a religion other than Islam risks being put to death.

5. In Afghanistan women are not allowed by some groups to be educated, in Saudi Arabia a woman may not drive a car, and girls in some countries will be 'married off' by their families to much older men without their consent. In Western Europe, young teenage girls will sometimes be taken back to Pakistan and to other territories to be married against their will, their relatives claiming that they are acting as God wishes.

Many committed Jews, Christians and Muslims would condemn these acts and say that they were a perversion of religion – but this claim demands that there be a way of separating acts done from religious motivations that are good from those that are bad. If there is no way of segregating good and bad religion, there is no way of separating those claims supposedly coming from God and those that may actually be claimed to come from God. This is particularly so when it is admitted that God may direct people through personal religious experience or conscience as well as through Holy Texts, for instance. Any fanatic may then use the cloak of religious allegiance to justify their actions, no matter how heinous.

What is significant, surprising and depressing about the examples listed above is that few Muslims, Christians and Jews are or were willing to stand against members of their own faith and to proclaim loudly and strongly 'This is wrong.' Instead they remained silent, and silence in the presence of injustice needs to be condemned in the strongest possible terms. Leaders of religious groups who remain silent should be subject to condemnation. The Christian Churches have, very occasionally, apologized for the wrongs committed by them in the past but, too often, they have remained silent and refused to recognize their own complicity in injustice and oppression. This is not only a moral but also a religious breakdown. Failure to stand against bad religion is a moral and religious failure. When supposedly good religion fails to stand against bad religion it must be judged as complicit and should be condemned accordingly. Muslims remained largely silent about the massacres in Darfur or the killing of Christians in Nigeria and elsewhere because they did not want to condemn fellow Muslims. Too few Jews have stood up against the actions of the Israeli government in the West Bank. Hardly any Christians challenged the crusades or the ways in which Muslims were demonized (Francis of Assisi is a heroic counter-example). The claim to represent good religion must be denied to those who allow bad religion to be practised by their own members and leaders without condemnation.

Of course, there are occasional voices who speak out against abuses from within their own communities, but these brave individuals are often oppressed and persecuted by their fellow religionists. It is often a lonely and isolated path to take.

One of the problems with Plato's and Socrates' solution to the Euthyphro dilemma is that it argues for an independent standard of goodness against which God can be judged. Bertrand Russell uses this as an argument against the existence of God: if there is an absolute standard of goodness independent of God, God is no longer supreme. Plato thought that his idea of god, the Demiurge (which means craftsman), could be judged to be good against an independent standard – the Form or absolute idea of The Good. Plato held that the Forms of Justice, Beauty and The Good (note that these are written with a capital letter) existed beyond time and space and were part of the very structure of the universe. Today few people are Platonists and, instead, many maintain that ideas like justice, beauty and goodness are entirely culturally relative. In today's postmodern world many hold that there is no meta-narrative, no single way of interpreting a text or understanding a painting, and that all supposed 'absolute' values are the creation of human society. If this view is taken, then Plato and Socrates are wrong – there is no absolute standard against which God can be judged. This apparently leads to the view that there can be no absolute standard against which good and bad religion can be judged. However, this pessimistic and negative conclusion can be argued against by appeal to Plato's foremost pupil – Aristotle.

4

Good and Bad

One approach to distinguishing 'good' from 'bad' has been to develop normative ethical systems, moral philosophies to account for the meaning of the terms and to describe a process for judging what actions each could apply to in a given situation. A number of different moral philosophies have been proposed over time and none is universally accepted. However, they may offer insight into this debate. Not forgetting that the whole business of judging religions according to independent moral standards is likely to be problematic, as discussed in the previous chapter, if the commands of a religion differ markedly from what most moral philosophies would argue to be good actions, this could be a starting point from which to judge those commands.

Happiness?

In the West the dominant moral philosophy is that of Utilitarianism. Many versions of this system have been proposed, but they mostly descend from the writings of Jeremy Bentham, an English radical lawyer and philosopher of the early nineteenth century. Bentham considered standards of law and morality in nineteenth-century Britain to be somewhat arbitrary, based on the traditions of the feudal system and the Anglican Church and, in many cases, arcane and irrational. He proposed revising the British legal system and beginning a public debate over standards of morality according to a new, areligious and purely rational system. He started with a claim from Greek Hedonism – 'nature has placed mankind under two sovereign masters, the pursuit of pleasure and the avoidance of pain' – and moved from this basic assumption of natural individual hedonism to his Utilitarian maxim, 'always act so as to produce the greatest happiness for the greatest number of people', or social hedonism. For Bentham, an action that produces happiness is a good action and conversely, an action that causes pain is a bad one.

Needless to say, an early problem lay in defining and measuring happiness and pain. Bentham argued that 'all things being equal, poetry is as good as pushpin', thus disregarding the long-established belief that the highest part of human nature is the reason, which should dominate the emotions and the animal appetites. If pleasure gained from good food or sex is on an equal footing to that gained from intellectual endeavour, people of all types and abilities can be judged on equal terms. No one person's pleasure potential is greater than any other's, and thus each can count as one in any calculation. This suited Bentham's radical belief in democracy well and would, if applied, have led to law that pleased the common majority rather than served an elite, as had traditionally been the case. Unfortunately, regarding all forms of pleasure is likely to lead to decisions that maximize those that have traditionally been seen as 'base', totally ignoring the 'higher' pleasures that are hard won and available to the few, not the many. A society run on Benthamite utilitarian lines is likely to invest in football stadiums and multiplex cinemas while closing down libraries and theatres. Moreover, if such a society is really trying to maximize pleasure of whatever sort, its legal system is likely to favour what people want rather than stand up for principles of right and justice against the baying demands of the press. Bentham's radical system was supposed to create a fairer world, but it would probably have just replaced the tyranny of the upper classes with the tyranny of the proletariat since so much today depends on the wishes of the majority (this was, incidentally, one reason why Plato had no regard for democracy, because 'the will of the people' ruled rather than what was right, just and good).

Nevertheless, Benthamite Utilitarianism has been influential, and versions of it have inspired public policy across Western countries seeking to demonstrate that they are free from religious control. The general principle that actions that produce happiness are good and those that produce pain are bad is accepted by most people. In many quarters democracy, the belief that every person is of equal worth and has an interest in decision making, is an unquestioned orthodoxy. This is despite the problems that follow on from democracy and social hedonism, chiefly the difficulty of taking any unpopular action, even when such is necessary to the long-term success or even survival of those affected. Consider the threats posed by inaction on environmental change, by failing to rebuild and replace power stations, by failing to invest in road, rail and other infrastructure projects, by ignoring overseas political or commercial threats. And yet it is almost impossible for democratic governments to raise taxes and make and enforce difficult policy changes on these issues in normal circumstances. This is because ordinary people weigh up the certain short-term personal pleasures of inaction against the uncertain future pleasures for their children of action, and opt for inaction every time. Perhaps Bentham was right in accepting the principle that people are essentially hedonists – but too optimistic in believing that they could be functioning social hedonists without much more education and help than they are ever likely to get.

It is not surprising, therefore, that today in the West many people look on religion with suspicion. With the prevailing utilitarian ethic, any system that proposes that people should do things that make them unhappy now, even for the promise of eternal gain in heaven, is counter-cultural. Does this make most religion 'bad'?

From the earliest days of Utilitarianism, refinements to Bentham's basic system have been suggested. John Stuart Mill, Bentham's godson, resisted equating all forms of pleasure and stood up for the existence of 'higher' intellectual pleasures and 'lower' physical or emotional ones. In this way utilitarian calculations could still support investment in the arts, in a principled justice system and in long-term political projects, but the side effect was that the principle of equality of persons was undermined.

Mill's system was, in the end, not dissimilar to that proposed by Immanuel Kant, which suggested that moral actions should begin in reason and end in rational satisfaction. For both Mill and Kant, the right action could produce immediate personal pain but would be justified either by 'higher' longer-term personal pleasure or by the pleasure of others and personal satisfaction in having done the right thing.

By these standards many religious commands could be judged good. Religious ways of living may demand personal sacrifice (modest dress, giving to charity, fasting, pilgrimage, prayer, asceticism, celibacy and so on), but these are all recommended as routes to long-term personal pleasures (or the avoidance of long-term personal pains!). Acts of self-sacrifice could also, arguably, be justified in the context of the feeling of satisfaction at having saved others and a possible 'higher' eternal reward. Most regular religious ways of living may not, therefore, conflict with a version of the dominant utilitarian ethic, yet it is clear that some do.

Extreme religious practices, such, as self-flagellation, physical mutilation, forcing children to live isolated monastic lives against their will, seeking martyrdom, forcibly converting or killing members of other faiths and traditions, cannot be reconciled with a definition of 'good' derived from happiness-producing and pain-avoiding behaviour. Such practices seem irrational and destructive. In fact they are rarely directed by clear passages in holy text or open revelations from religious figures. In most cases they derive from supposed commands from God issued through a personal religious experience to a charismatic leader, or through an idiosyncratic reading of text promoted by such a leader.

Perhaps because most religions propose ways of living that combine the reasonable with those practices that are on the borders of rational explanation, 'divine command' theories (see pp. 40–41) have been popular within religious communities and societies, while moral philosophies, even where they offer rational support to much the same ways of living, have been resisted. If goodness depends on what God commands, there can be no question about God's supremacy, such as there would be if any independent moral standard were admitted. Nor can there be any question about the supremacy of religious authorities, which are needed to communicate God's commands given the inadequacy of human reason.

The dangers inherent in divine command theories of ethics have been outlined in the previous chapter. Such a rationale can be used to claim that extreme religious practices, such as female circumcision, whipping oneself or submitting to slow starvation or poisoning, are good. In the cases of both extreme practices and those usually seen as less extreme, the only happiness produced derives from fitting in with expectations and the tenuous promise of heavenly reward, the latter usually reliant on texts quoted out of context or personal revelations to charismatic religious leaders of the past. It is true that such practices may also be argued to foster self-control, which can be seen as a good; but, arguably, less extreme ways could be found to achieve this objective. Where then should the line be drawn? How can extreme practices be distinguished from those arguably less extreme and more common, and present in most forms of religion? How can good religion be distinguished from bad religion when it comes to religious practice?

If both divine command theories and judging religious practices according to an independent rational standard of good and bad are fraught with difficulty, is there another way forward when it comes to judging good and bad religion?

Aristotle to the rescue

As suggested earlier (see p. 23), there is a tendency for philosophers, whether theist or atheist, to try to resolve problems by looking back to ancient Greek philosophy for both ideas and authority to support assumptions. The achievement of Greek thinkers such as Plato and Aristotle were immense and their insights may be useful in this case.

If there needs to be a way of separating good and bad religion, there needs to be a way of separating those commands that are supposed to come from God and those that may actually do so. Plato's attempt to solve the problem fails as few today hold that there is a single, absolute standard of 'The Good' against which supposed commands of God or religious imperatives or practices can be judged.

Aristotle rejected the idea that there is any single idea of what is good, which all good things resemble. This was Plato's claim when he held that all good things in some way participate in or resemble the absolute Form of The Good. Instead, Aristotle argued that a thing is good in so far as it fulfils its nature. The universe is, as Ludwig Wittgenstein observed, 'everything that is'; it is what it is and therefore fulfils its nature and is 'good' when seen in its entirety; however, we experience the universe only in part; we are limited by our time and place and by our human perspective.[1] Elements of the universe, whether vegetable, animal or mineral, may be more or less fulfilled (good) at any particular time or place. Everything in the universe, according to Aristotle, every plant, person or landscape, has a particular nature. A wombat has the potential to be, at different times and places, an embryo, a baby wombat in its mother's pouch, a young wombat, an adult wombat, a decrepit elderly wombat and a dead, decaying corpse. For Aristotle, at some of these stages its wombat-nature and potentials are more fulfilled – it is able to do more of the things that are distinctively wombat – than at others. The same could be said of an oak tree. It has the potential to be acorn, sapling, tree and pile of logs, and is more fully an oak tree at some points than others. The same could be said of all elements of the universe – wombats, seagulls, oak trees and gladioli. Goodness can be judged according to the degree in which the thing is fulfilling its nature at a given point.

Everything in the universe has potentiality built into it, and this potential includes the possibility of being destroyed or dying before this full potential is reached. Every sperm has the potential to fertilize an egg and to become a new individual depending on

---

1 Ludwig Wittgenstein, *Tractatus Logico-Philosophicus*, 2nd edition, London: Routledge, 2001, p. 1.

the animal in question, but the vast majority of sperm never fertilize an egg. Even when the egg is fertilized, most embryos do not
grow to be adults. Adult frogs produce vast quantities of frog-
spawn throughout their lives, but two adult frogs only need to
produce two more adult frogs throughout their entire life for the
population of frogs to remain stable. Nevertheless, the potential
to become a full adult frog is present in every single frog egg, even
though this is not realized in the vast majority of cases. Every tree
produces countless seeds, each with the full potential to become a
full-grown tree in its own right, but hardly any seeds will fulfil this
potential. The fact, therefore, that potentiality is built into something does not mean that this potential is realized.

Something is good, for Aristotle, when it realizes its potential –
when its 'formal cause' (and for Aristotle this means its nature)
is realized and it becomes what it is capable of being. So a good
seagull is a seagull that reaches the potential that all seagulls
share. A good wombat reaches the full potential of being a wombat; a good star fulfils the potential inbuilt into what it means to
be a star. Something is good, therefore, not – as Plato argued –
because it resembles some abstract idea of The Good but because
it fulfils its nature. Aristotle was the first Western scientist – the
first to study animals and plants to seek to understand their nature. Today he might well have been a geneticist or an expert in
animal behaviour, but he would have studied animals and plants
to seek to understand their true potential – what they are capable
of being at their best. If one is going to study a particular plant
or animal, one would seek to study those examples that are the
best of their type. One can then understand which examples fail
to fulfil their true potential – fail to be what their nature intends
them to be. We can say that a seagull without a wing is defective
because we know from observing seagulls that they are meant to
have two wings and be able to fly. We can say an oak tree that
has become twisted and distorted when it was young will never
reach the full potential of which an oak tree is capable.

Just as plants and animals all have distinct natures depending
on the type of animal or plant they are, so Aristotle held that all
human beings share a common human nature. Humans are not

seagulls or oak trees or wombats. Human beings are, necessarily, part of the species homo sapiens. Humans may have different skin, eye and hair colour, some may be short and others tall, some may have some aptitudes more than others, but they are all human beings – they all share in a common human nature. When a baby is born it has the potential to grow into a child, then into a teenager and then into an adult. As an adult it has a wide range of potentialities that it may or may not fulfil. Parents cherish their children, protect them and seek to help them to fulfil their potential. The children go to school, learn about relationships, develop individual skills, compete with others and go through the sometimes painful process of growing into adulthood. Tragically, some children die young, and their potential is never realized. Part of the tragedy of losing a child is the recognition that all the potential that was present in the young person is cut short and will never be fulfilled. Also many adults fail to realize their full potential and remain unfulfilled. Defining precisely what human nature is and what it means to fulfil human potential is not easy, but nevertheless this potential is real and exists.

If human nature can be defined, and goodness lies in fulfilling that nature, it is a relatively simple matter to describe the sort of actions and practices that would be good and those that would be bad. There have been many attempts to describe 'natural laws', principles encouraging or prohibiting actions on the basis that they either support human fulfilment or detract from it. Different philosophers have understood human nature differently, and so although in theory natural law is a single absolute system that would apply equally to all people, in practice its imperatives are far from clear. Nevertheless, it remains a promising source of standards against which to judge religions and religious practices.

This is because the paradigm (world view) out of which Aristotle developed the basic theory of natural law is compatible with the paradigms that gave rise to the major world religions. So much is this the case that Christians, Jews and Muslims in particular have on occasion used Aristotelian moral philosophy to support and extend their own moral codes. For Aristotle, the universe is ordered and governed by consistent principles, and the human senses and mind are able to understand it and discover those principles to a large extent. The order in the universe and the unique position of human beings support belief that the universe may have had an origin, may have been designed and indeed may have been formed around the needs and wants of human beings in some way. Although Aristotle did not accept that human beings can know anything beyond the universe that we can experience, he proposed arguments that point to the existence of a 'prime mover', a 'divine designer', which may be equated with a single omnipotent creator God.

In the thirteenth century CE Thomas Aquinas saw in Aristotle a philosophical system that was compatible with monotheistic faith and might provide the foundations of a stronger, systematic approach to Christianity. Aquinas' approach was developed and later adopted by the Roman Catholic Church at the Council of Trent. Aquinas was one of the first Western Christian scholars to have access to the writings of Aristotle since the collapse of the Roman Empire and the destruction, by Goths and Vandals, of most of the libraries in Europe. His tutor at the University of Paris, Alexander of Hales, had made translations into Latin from manuscripts held in Arabic at the University of Córdoba (see below), and had brought them back to Paris a decade before Aquinas arrived there.

For Aquinas, though Aristotle was right in his conclusion that human beings cannot know anything in the ordinary way beyond the limits of experience, revelation through the Bible enabled human beings to know that God created the universe good (for instance, Gen. 1.10) and made human beings '*in his own image*' (Gen. 1.28) with the ability to understand and use creation to his glory. The arguments Aristotle proposed as pointing to the existence of a prime mover or divine designer provided useful support to faith in a single creator God based on revelation.

Though the first Christian scholar to use Aristotle for centuries, Aquinas was not the first religious scholar to see and use Aristotle's potential. While Europe was in the dark ages, Islam was on the rise. After the death of the Prophet, Islamic armies spread Islam across the whole of North Africa and into Spain. As the armies advanced across Egypt they captured Alexandria and with it the great library. One might have expected the Islamic armies to have destroyed this library, but the Qur'an exhorts Muslims to learning. The books were carefully transported back from Alexandria to the great University of Baghdad and, in due course, to the newer but equally significant Islamic university in Córdoba in Spain. Here the books were translated into Arabic, and the wisdom of the Greeks became available to Islamic scholars. This led to an incredible Islamic renaissance of learning, to the finest medicine, astronomy, mathematics, philosophy and theology being developed. Muslim scholars saw in Aristotle a philosophical system that was compatible with – indeed enriched – their monotheistic faith. Of particular concern to this discussion is the use made of Aristotle's work by Islamic philosophers such as Ibn Sina and Ibn Rushd, who argued that God had to be one and that God was outside time and space. This was an identical conclusion to that arrived at by the Early Christian Church Fathers, who wanted to ensure that the Christian God was not seen as one of the gods, another god like the Greek and Roman gods, but as the one true God. These gods were anthropomorphic – in time and space. They had petty jealousies and rivalries and competed with each other. They had sexual relations with each other and with human beings and were capricious. Christians, Muslims and Jews were clear that the one God whom they worshipped was very different from this. God was beyond time and space, absolutely unlike anything in the universe. The Jewish philosopher Maimonides expressed this well when he said that God could not be spoken about – 'I am that I am' (the reply given by God to Moses from the burning bush, when Moses asked for the name of God) came closest to expressing God's reality. God could not change, God had no potential – God was pure actuality and was perfect in that God perfectly fulfilled the nature of God.

For both Aquinas and his Muslim predecessors, moral imperatives were revealed by religion, along with specific religious practices, which together would enable people to do God's will. Yet moral imperatives, unlike specific religious practices, could also be discovered through the rational analysis of human experience according to the method of Aristotelian natural law. Standards of right and wrong, good and bad are thus implicit in the way that God created the universe and all the things in it. They emanate from God and are thus not independent of him or transcendent but are universal, apply across the boundaries of religion or culture and do not change with time or place. Therefore in Aristotelian natural law there may be a solution to the problem of how to judge religion and religious practices as good or bad. Natural law may provide universal standards that can apply across the major religious traditions and that may be accepted by atheists, but that do not suggest that God is being judged against an independent standard that may make him subservient and not worthy of worship.

Religion and human flourishing

Aristotle had argued that human beings shared a common human nature and, if this was so, then Christian, Muslim and Jewish philosophers argued that what God wanted above all was that human beings should fulfil the God-given potential they all shared. Religion was about helping people to become fully human – to become what they were capable of being at their best; to fulfil their full human potential. This approach was developed clearly in Islam but, even more so, in Christianity, by Thomas Aquinas.

Aquinas argued that although God's will is free and God can will whatever God wants, what is morally right or wrong is based on the shared nature of human beings. God creates human nature and, in so doing, determines what will contribute to human flourishing and what will lead people away from fulfilling their potential. God is therefore the author of morality in that God creates humans with the nature they have, but the commands in the Bible are not arbitrary commands – rather they are examples in practice of those actions that dehumanize or those actions that tend to make us more fully human. This has become known as the natural-law tradition of ethics.

Aquinas, however, in order to emphasize God's freedom, allows God to command actions that go against general moral rules, but these are exceptions and unusual – normally morality is based firmly on understanding what it means to live a fulfilled human life. Aristotle put forward key cardinal virtues: courage, temperance, wisdom and justice. These were also accepted by Plato, Cicero and Augustine of Hippo. To these Thomas Aquinas, writing in the thirteenth century, added the theological virtues of faith, hope and charity. Virtue ethics is not so much interested in the question 'What should I do?' but rather in the question 'What sort of person should I become?' This has more to do with character and the nature of what it is to be human than with the rights and wrongs of specific actions. Good religion takes character formation seriously – it is about, as we saw in the previous chapter, a transformation of human beings, not simply a matter of belonging to a religious group.

Virtue ethics stems from natural law – but instead of laying down a series of actions which a person should not do (for instance, the Ten Commandments), it focuses on people developing the virtues. Aristotle argued that to become virtuous needed constant practice (just as an athlete had to train in order to become fit), so a person could only become virtuous by attending to their actions in every small aspect of their lives in order to develop patterns of virtuous behaviour. In every action one should be asking, 'Is this action making me more just, more courageous and more virtuous?' Temperance is the Aristotelian mean – it calls people to live by the middle way, avoiding extremes. Temperance calls on people to avoid extremes of conduct. A small amount of wine may be beneficial, none may impair one's pleasure and too much may lead one out of control. Foolhardiness in war may lead to unnecessary loss of life but cowardice will lead to defeat – so bravery is the mean between these extremes. Some sport may be a good thing but none will mean your body is out of condition; and if life is all sport, the balance is lost. Life is multi-dimensional, and to live life to the full means keeping a proper balance between many different aspects. This is part of cultivating the virtues – fostering a balanced life.

Religions teach people to reorder their priorities, to look at life in a new way, to challenge the world's priorities and to seek to live life accountable to God or some supreme reality. They may differ in terms of their detailed teaching but they all affirm the importance of right conduct and the danger of behaving in ways that lead them away from fulfilling their core potential. Confucius, who lived within 60 years of Plato but in a totally different culture, emphasized the importance of *ren* – conduct worthy or becoming of a human being – and warned of the danger of other forms of conduct. Buddhism, Sikhism and Hinduism all do the same. There is an admirable quality to many who take religion seriously, and it can be seen in the practice of the virtues and a life that shows goodness at a deep level – this does not depend on a particular set of creeds or dogmas but on a quality of what it is to be human at its best. Florence Nightingale, Mahatma Gandhi, Guru Nanak, Martin Luther King and Nelson Mandela did not share a single set of beliefs but they exemplify in different ways what it is to be a human being at its best.

God, on this view, wants human beings to develop to their full potential, and the aim of human life is to actualize this God-given potential. Human nature stems from God and God is, therefore, the author of human nature. Even religions that do not explicitly affirm God, such as Buddhism, recognized the cultivation of the virtues as being essential and the practice of 'mindfulness' is a matter of becoming aware of all one's action, thoughts and responses so that one acts rightly rather than according to instinct. It is a matter of individuals establishing control over themselves so that they are self-consciously acting to cultivate the virtues. Those actions that help people to realize their full potential are good and those actions that diminish or damage human beings and lead them away from their full potential are bad. The understanding of potentiality will, of course, vary between those with a religious and a secular orientation. Aristotle himself did not believe in any idea of life after death (except in one disputed text that most modern commentators believe was not written by him). His view of human potentiality would, therefore, share much in common with modern secular humanists who would see human potential being confined to this life, while most religious people would hold that human potential finds its fulfilment after death in some post-mortem existence.

On this view, religion is about helping individuals to fulfil their true potential – to become what they are capable of being at their very best. Actions are wrong that diminish us and lead us away from our potential, while actions are good or virtuous that lead us towards the potential that all human beings share. All religions claim that religion is central to helping people to fulfil their potential, and a life lived just for self, just for material satisfaction, is a pale reflection of what a human being is capable of becoming. Across the world religions of different sorts challenge the widely accepted orthodoxy that life is about money, sex, technology, consumerism, putting self first, seeking to accumulate power, influence and reputations. Religion argues that there is more to life than this and that an exclusive pursuit of these goals leads people away from their true potential.

Plato argued that the highest duty of a human being is 'care of their soul' – by which he meant caring for the depth of what a person really is at its deepest level. Many actions damage human beings at this deepest level – they cause them to become more like animals than human beings and, in so doing, deny their real potential. Human beings are more than just animals concerned to satisfy their instincts. Human beings are free to make choices and to become what they are capable of being at their very best. Socrates once asked whether it was better to suffer harm or to inflict harm – is it better to be tortured or to be a torturer? While the prospect of being tortured is appalling, Socrates maintained that those carrying out torture damaged themselves more than those who were tortured since the person who carries out the torture damages their soul or, to put it another way, damages themselves at the deepest level possible. If the soul is immortal, if the essential part of what it is to be a human being survives death and has to account for the life it has lived, what matters most is not what happens to a human being's body but how they have cared for their soul (which, to repeat, can be understood as the deepest part of their self, which will survive death). Almost every religion affirms this crucial insight and, in essence, it is at the heart of all religion.

After the terrorist attacks on London on 7/7, Heythrop College (which is the specialist theology and philosophy college of the University of London) decided to launch the first BA in Abrahamic Studies in Europe. This focused on the three great monotheistic religions – Judaism, Christianity and Islam. The course was to be taught by practising members of the different faith communities. In preparing for this degree, the college brought over from the University of Qom in Iran a leading Shiite Islamic philosopher and theologian and, because office space was tight, he shared an office with an Orthodox Jew. There are few institutions in the world where two people from such diverse backgrounds worked in such close proximity, but what united them was the quality of who they were as human beings. Their gentleness, openness, willingness to listen and always to see the good in others was clear to all. Their credal beliefs were radically different but who they were as human beings was not. It is this towards which Aristotle's approach to being human and fulfilling human potential points. Religion at its best seeks to develop human potential and, so the religious perspective on life argues, this potential cannot solely be explained in material terms. Feuerbach, Marx, Freud and Dawkins are wrong – there is more to life than science can explain and it is this 'more', this greater capacity to be fully human, that religion seeks to make manifest and towards which it points.

Immanuel Kant made a similar point: he argued that animals have what he called 'empirical souls' – they are dominated by instinct and innate desires and have little capacity for rational thought beyond seeking what is in their own self-interest. God, Kant argued, was wholly rational and, in giving human beings both rationality and freedom, wanted human beings to act according to reason. Humans are a mixture – partly animal and partly rational. Kant expressed this by saying that humans have both rational and empirical souls, but by this he did not mean that human beings have two separate substances dwelling inside them. Rather he was pointing to two aspects of human personality – the one is focused on animal desires and instincts and the other is rational. The task of human life is to bring the animal desires that all human beings share under control and to make them subject to reason. Kant did not believe there was any way of proving the existence of God, but the rationality and order of the universe we experience makes it reasonable to postulate the existence of God, human freedom and immortality[2] to explain it. He sought to develop religion 'within the limits of reason alone' (cf. pp. 83–85), but this did not mean that religion can be reduced to rational categories – there is more to religion than this but, nevertheless, reason is an important part of what it means to be human, and the exercise of reason is part of the human potentiality everyone shares.

International law

Aristotle's influence has been profound, not just on religion but on the secular world as well. After the Second World War, Nazi leaders were placed on trial for the obscene actions that led to the Holocaust. At the Nuremburg war crimes trial the lawyers for the Nazi leaders argued that they were simply obeying orders. Germany as a country was internationally recognized by the League of Nations and other countries around the world, and Hitler's government was similarly recognized. In Germany, Jews were regarded as subhuman, and killing Jews, homosexuals, gypsies and those with disabilities was considered a good thing. This idea had, in fact, a long history, some

---

2 Kant's tombstone read 'two things ever fill me with awe: the starry sky above me and the moral law within me'. He saw the existence of morality as an extension and confirmation of the existence of order in the universe. Order and morality he saw as satisfactory grounds for postulating the existence of God, freedom of the will and immortality. None of these three can be proved, but if the universe is really ordered, as our moral sense indicates that it is, then it makes sense to accept that freedom is real, that moral laws have an origin and purpose (in God) and that a reward and/or punishment exists to vindicate the existence of these laws.

scientists both in the United Kingdom and the United States arguing for genetic selection on Darwinian lines to improve the human gene-pool. In Germany these ideas were actually put into practice, but it would be a mistake to think that these were solely German ideas. Germany decided to apply these ideas and felt there was good reason to do so (however horrific this may seem to others today). Those, therefore, within Germany who obeyed the laws of German society could not, it was argued, be condemned for doing so. The law is supreme and, within Nazi Germany, the law dictated that Jews, homosexuals, gypsies and others did not deserve to live or, at least, should be prevented from breeding. The defence lawyers argued that the prosecution lawyers at the Nuremburg trials were simply applying the victors' morality to judge the vanquished. The United States, Britain and other allies had won the war and were imposing their ideas of morality onto the defeated Germany, and had no right to do so. The Nazis should be acquitted as they had been faithful servants of the Nazi state and could only be judged by the laws of their own state. Effectively this was rejecting any absolute standard of morality and instead claiming (as many do today) that morality is entirely relative. This was a persuasive position but it was rejected. Instead it was held that the Nazi leaders were guilty of 'crimes against humanity' – they had carried out acts that went against what it was to be human. This was directly based on Aristotle's philosophy and the tradition that followed from it. Certain actions go against the common nature that all human beings share and, therefore, need to be condemned and judged as wrong.

The international criminal court in The Hague continues this tradition: certain leaders are arrested and arraigned before the court for 'crimes against humanity'. It does not matter, it is held, what the laws of a particular country may be: certain actions, such as genocide, are wrong in and of themselves because they go against what it is to be human, against 'human nature'. Those who seek to defend themselves by saying, that 'in our country genocide is morally acceptable' are condemned. Aquinas suggested that 'every human law has just so much of the nature of law as is derived from the law of nature. But if in any point it deflects from the law of nature, it is no longer a law but a perversion of law.'[3] The principle of international law is heavily influenced by the Aristotelian claim that certain actions can be judged to be wrong because they go against the common nature that all human beings share. International law is, therefore, an attempt at codifying natural law. William Blackstone, the eighteenth-century jurist, wrote:

> This law of nature, being co-eval with (part of) mankind and dictated by God himself, is of course superior in obligation to any other. It is binding over all the globe, in all countries, and at all times: no human laws are of any validity, if contrary to this; and such of them as are valid derive all their force, and all their authority . . . from this original.[4]

Almost every country in the world accepts the existence and authority of international (natural) law. One of the very few exceptions is the United States, which refuses to allow US citizens to be judged by an international court. This is not because it considers the basis for the international condemnation to be wrong, but because it is unwilling for any US personnel to be arraigned before a non-US court as, of course, in military activities in some parts of the world some US personnel might be considered to be guilty under international law, even though they may have been obeying orders. It is perhaps ironic that the United States stands against the principle of natural law when the language of the Declaration of Independence and the Constitution appeals to this very principle on numbers of occasions. The idea that all men are born equal and entitled to pursue the natural ends of life, liberty and happiness is the basis of the 'American Dream'. The Australian government maintained the same stance as that of the United States with regard to international law and

---

3 *Summa Theologiae I–II*, Q.95, A.II.
4 William Blackstone, *Commentaries on the Laws of England*, with an introduction by Stanley N. Katz, Chicago: University of Chicago Press, 1979, p. 41.

international courts until 2008, when a new Labour government was elected that agreed to be bound by their rulings and to allow their citizens to be arraigned at The Hague.

Conclusion

This book will contend that Aristotelian philosophy offers a partial solution to the problem of devising standards against which to judge religion and religious practices. As has been explained, the natural-law approach is compatible with the major world religions and indeed has been used by them in the past to extend and enrich their philosophies of religion and moral philosophies. Further, the approach may be acceptable to atheist philosophers as well. Although not universally accepted, most normative ethical systems rely on defining good and bad in relation to what it means to be a fulfilled human being. For Utilitarians, being a fulfilled human being is about being 'happy' and free from 'pain', howsoever those states are defined. For Kant, being human is about being free and rational. For Aquinas, it is about cultivating the virtues, living peacefully, acquiring wisdom and passing it on to the next generation – and giving thanks to God for the opportunity. If theology is really debates over the grammar and vocabulary religious people should use when referring to the divine, then it might be concluded that moral philosophy is similar. Different thinkers define human nature in different ways, but in the end it might be concluded that they are pointing to similar things.

It seems that 'good religion' must aim to foster human flourishing, to help human beings to develop their full potential, howsoever this may be defined. Most religions and most moral philosophies hold that human nature is common across all cultures. Further, that human beings were created by God or otherwise exist with the same potentialities and subject to the same principles of right and wrong. Clearly there is no agreement about precisely how human nature should be defined or what exactly is right or what wrong, but nevertheless there is a commonality that could be grounds for a discussion across the divisions of theism and between theists and atheists. Willingness to engage in such a discussion could be a criterion for judging a religion 'good', along with the acceptance that there exist examples of individuals who have fulfilled their full potential, good people – within all societies and all religions. Good religion would therefore speak to all people and aim to foster human potential – promote flourishing and the cultivation of the virtues. Good religion can be seen to help people to develop into individuals where compassion, patience, love, pity, the ability to forgive, an absence of anger and humility are all present. Where these are absent, bad religion may have taken hold.

PART TWO

A Way Forward

So far this book has set out the challenge involved in distinguishing 'good' religion from 'bad' religion by describing four
particular issues.

First, there was the issue of loyalty among theists, who often
feel bound to group together in the face of attack by atheists and
defend religion, even when what is being attacked is hardly recognizable as the form of life (cultural milieu) to which they belong. Thus atheism may have the effect of fostering bad religion
by creating out of supporters of good religion defenders of less
admirable faith and practice. This book has suggested that atheists should recognize that religion is not a consistent, monolithic
phenomenon and be prepared to differentiate between good religion and bad religion, targeting their criticism more accurately
so that supporters of good religion and atheists might actually be
on the same side in attacking bad religion.

Second, there was the issue of truth in religion, which is not to
be reduced to what may be verified or even falsified and cannot
easily be judged according to what may or may not be acceptable
to those outside the religious community. Religions try to reveal
truth beyond the material and what is normally accessible to human beings, and must communicate through a range of aesthetic
experiences, not just through clear statements or equations that
apply only to definite phenomena. There was therefore a discussion of the difficulty of using truth as a standard against which
to judge religion when religious beliefs and practices defy normal standards of proof and rationality. An anti-realist approach
to truth in religion was described and evaluated, but it seemed

inadequate to express what religions claim to be about and likely to promote a relativism that would make the task of judging religion to be good or bad impossible.

Third, there was a discussion of the difficulty of judging a religion as good or bad when most religions claim that those very standards emanate from their God. The so-called Euthyphro dilemma, which suggests that arguing that good and bad depend on God is actually a weak position, was described, but so was the difficulty of religions accepting the existence of independent, universal standards of good and bad against which religious beliefs and practices could be judged. This gave rise to a problem to which the next chapter suggested a solution.

Fourth, the possibility of using independent, universal standards to judge religion was explored. The existence of several different philosophical approaches to the nature of goodness and badness was noted and certain commonalities between these approaches highlighted, namely the relationship between goodness and fulfilment of human nature (howsoever that is defined) and the importance of rationality in that nature. The possibility of basing criteria with which to judge religion on Aristotelian philosophy was then considered. Aristotle's world view and method has the benefit both of being compatible with religious world views and traditional methods of moral philosophy, and of being acceptable to many atheists as well. It could provide universal standards by which to judge religion that are arguably not independent of God, thus avoiding the problem highlighted in Chapter 3 on the Euthyphro dilemma.

The remainder of this book will consider if and how these broadly Aristotelian criteria might be used to judge religions, and how good religion and bad religion might be manifested in various respects. How would a good religion use authority and texts, what would be its relationship with science and justice, how would it relate to different groups in society such as women, the disabled or those of other religions, and what place would individual freedom have? Similarly, what would be the mark of bad religion in the use of authority and text,

in the treatment of science and justice, in the handling of difference in society and in attitudes to individual freedom?
These criteria may offer a way forward and, while they may
not be conclusive, or polished, as described here they may be a
starting point for discussions.

5

Authority

The word 'religion' comes from the Latin word for 'to bind to-gether'. Religion is therefore that which brings individuals to-gether into a group, that which contains people or to which they conform. All major religions have power structures, hierarchies whose role it is to ensure that doctrine and practice are communicated and monitored effectively. All those who communicate doctrine must be authorized by someone senior, and all forms of religious practice, including moral behaviour, must be judged by a central authority. Religious authorities are, in practice, a central part of the bindings that hold members of a religion together; they are what make a religion a religion.

Religious authorities seek to bind members of a religion by and around the truth that that religion claims to possess. Religions need authorities or they cannot function; without them there are just disparate individuals with many varying ideas and customs. Yet authority can only be validly exercised if it is in the service of truth; if the truth is questioned, so the authority of those who seek to bind people to and by it will be questioned. Power and authority have an uneasy relationship, within religion as much as within other structures. With authority tends to come power, and power can confer a sense of authority, but it is certainly possible to possess and use power without proper authority – to abuse power. To use the power that comes from being part of a religious hierarchy knowingly to impose a false view of doctrine, beliefs and creeds cannot and must not be defended. Even though, therefore, it may not be possible to prove by reason that one set of religious beliefs is more true than another, nevertheless the issue of truth matters, and authority in religion is justified because of its claim that it is holding fast to what is claimed to be true.

Religion has often been a belonging system rather than a system of individual transformation. What mattered was to belong to a particular group, to participate and to be accepted by the group. This led to an 'us' and 'them' approach: 'We' are saved; 'they' are not. 'We' are destined for heaven; 'they' are destined for hell. When believing and belonging become the central parts of religion, authority tends to dominate. What becomes crucial is showing that one belongs by, for instance, attending services and submitting to the authority of the group, rather than the personal transformation that is the essence of good religion.

Religion has always been closely associated with authority – those with authority seeking to impose a single view on others to ensure orthodoxy. Religious groups seek to impose their authority on their members, sometimes for the best of reasons. They will exclude those members who do not accept the central authority or who refuse to conform. Exclusion is used as a weapon of social control. Each religion will feel that it alone has the truth and that those who dissent from this truth need to be corrected from their error and 'won for orthodoxy'. The long history of rejecting heresy and enforcing orthodoxy is based on the view that holding on to religious truth is of paramount importance. Religions tend to be associated with a single claim to truth, and each religious group is anxious to preserve fidelity to what it sees as ultimate truth. Almost any means can be seen as justifiable if truth is to be preserved. The view that heresy has no rights, a position that has been taken as justification for the suppression of any views not considered as orthodox, where what is orthodox are those beliefs communally accepted within a religious organization.

One of the most important eras that saw authority being misused to ensure conformity occurred at the end of the Islamic enlightenment period. After the death of the Prophet, Islamic armies spread across North Africa and into Spain. The great library of Alexandria was captured, but instead of it being destroyed as might have been expected with other invading armies, the Muslim conquerors preserved the books and took them back to Baghdad. The greatest Islamic centres of learning therefore had access to the works of the finest ancient Greek thinkers and, in particular, to Aristotle. This led to a tremendous Islamic renaissance in astronomy, medicine, philosophy and theology. Aristotle's works were used by philosophers such as Ibn Sina and Ibn Rushd (Averroës and Avicenna) to understand the nature of God. God was argued to be beyond time and spaceless, bodiless and radically other than anything in the universe of space and time. This, in turn, meant that language in the Qur'an that implied that God could change or had a body had to be reinterpreted and seen in metaphorical or allegorical terms. The Qur'an could not, therefore, be taken literally and had to be interpreted in the light of reason. The Qur'an was still held to be dictated by God but it could be read at different levels, and those trained in philosophy were held to be able to understand at a deeper level than those who did not have this training. This was seen as a threat by many who wanted the Qur'an to be taken literally as the divinely dictated word of God accessible to all, equally.

A popular movement rejecting the primacy of philosophy and reason spread across the Islamic world, which rapidly led to Islamic philosophy being effectively closed down from the end of the twelfth century. The books of many of the great Islamic philosophers were burnt. The authority of the Qur'an was seen as under threat from reason, and the reaction was an authoritarian one that still contributes to a particular way of reading the text that is intolerant of independent philosophical enquiry. Throughout the world today the focus of much Islamic education is on learning and reading the text of the Qur'an, and the issue of the complexity of interpretation tends to be confined to universities. Authority, therefore, has been imposed by many Islamic states and religious authorities to ensure obedience to the text. Indeed, some Muslim scholars proclaim that the Qur'an is not a created document – it is uncreated, part of God's essence and as timeless as God. Authority is needed to ensure that this view dominates and that credence is not given to alternative views that might challenge orthodoxy.

The early Christian Church spent four centuries seeking to agree on orthodoxy. Fierce debates were held between varieties of competing positions until at length, with the eventual authority of the Christian Roman Emperor, a single understanding of orthodoxy was enforced. Votes were taken at great Councils of Bishops of the Church. The majority vote became orthodoxy and dissenting voices were suppressed. Agreement was seen to ensure truth since God was held to have guided the Church towards agreement. What was agreed has come down to the present age in what is now Christian orthodoxy, and the Church devoted much of its long history to suppressing heresy. The authority of the Church was seen as paramount and dissent was suppressed in an often cruel and vicious manner. Those who challenged authority were subject to heresy trials and put to death, or excommunicated and told that they were destined for hell. The great split between the Western and Eastern Christian Churches in 1054 stemmed partly from issues of doctrine but equally significantly from the competing authoritarian powers of Rome and Constantinople – the New Rome as it was called. The issue was whose authority was paramount, the Patriarch in Constantinople or the Bishop of Rome? The actual issue that caused the rift was the '*filioque* clause', which had been inserted by Western Churches without the authority of any of the great Councils of the Church that agreed orthodoxy. The dispute concerning this clause purported to be about whether the Holy Spirit (the third person of the Trinity that is maintained by Christians) proceeds from God the Father alone or from God the Father and God the Son (the first two persons of the Christian Trinity). In practice, however, the real dispute was about whose authority dominated.

In the Middle Ages, political and religious authority combined to ensure orthodoxy within their respective spheres of influence. The power of the Church and the power of secular authorities came together to maintain a feudal system that endorsed a hierarchical approach to knowledge and to society. The King or

Queen stood at the summit of the secular apex of authority and the Pope at the summit of the religious apex. It was a powerful combination, and both power structures worked together to ensure that orthodoxy dominated and social order and obedience were maintained. Crusades were launched against dissenters who held to non-orthodox views. Hundreds of thousands were killed to ensure that the authority of the Church in Rome remained paramount.

The Inquisition was later employed, using torture to seek out dissidents suspected of heresy. The fear of the Inquisition was very great – almost anyone could be charged and few were acquitted. Denouncing someone else was often a sure way of deflecting heresy charges from oneself, and tens of thousands of supposed heretics and witches were condemned and burnt, often on the uncorroborated word of a single individual. By these harsh, brutal and inhuman means, the authority of the Church and, more locally, of the priest was enforced, so that it came to be considered almost unquestionable. What was more, the price for challenging orthodoxy was great both in this world and the next – heretics were assured of being punished eternally in hell. The combination of secular and Church authority thus made an almost irresistible combination.

The Protestant Reformation challenged the previous certainties proclaimed by the Church and started to erode the central authority of the Roman Church. The Bible had been translated from Latin into the vernacular, and with the rise of the middle classes and the invention of the printing press, more people began to read the Bible for themselves. The teaching of the Church was compared with the text of the Bible, and many Protestants considered that the authority of the Church and Rome was flawed. Wycliffe, Hus, Luther, Calvin and other Reformers rejected the authority and power of Rome, leading to the Protestant reformation sweeping across Europe – albeit itself giving rise to more dissent and splits. There was a rise in sects and small religious groups, each claiming its own authority and rejecting the authority of others. Different religious views were embraced by different states, and wars broke out across Europe that were partly political but also partly ideological as competing authorities sought to ensure that their own orthodoxy dominated.

This climate was to influence the newly discovered North America, to which many fled from the authority of religious persecution in their home countries. When America is described as 'the land of the free', the freedom that is perhaps most prominent is religious freedom – at least in theory. In practice, politics and religion in the United States are closely intertwined, and proclaimed loyalty to the (Christian) God and to the American state and the American flag are often seen as going hand in hand. The rise of Protestantism did not undermine authority. It simply introduced new and fragmented authority structures that competed with the older structures. Again, what was seen to matter was belonging to the 'right' group and thereby being justified. Authority was needed within each group to ensure orthodoxy and orthopraxy within the group.

The same has happened in Judaism within the last hundred years as many different branches have emerged, including Orthodox, Liberal and Reformed. Each branch has its own synagogues and authority structures. For instance, in Britain the authority of the Chief Rabbi is accepted by the Orthodox but not by Liberal or Reformed Jews. Tensions between these groups have been very great, one group often not recognizing the others as 'real' Jews. Most often the tensions arise around the authority given to the Torah and Talmud and how these are to be read. Different authorities have arisen within each group proclaiming the rightness of their own view and rejecting the authority of others. Reformed Judaism challenged Orthodox Judaism precisely on the issue of truth. Many rabbis rejected the prevailing orthodoxy, but their voices were not heard and they felt forced to form their own congregations and to buy or build different synagogues. The pains of this split are still felt within Judaism, the tensions between communities are still present. In an episode of the American TV series *The West Wing*, one of the President's senior staff members, who is Jewish, speaks to his rabbi about the death penalty. He quotes from the Torah, which clearly laid down the death penalty for various offences. The rabbi, however, replies as follows:

> It (The Torah) says a rebellious child can be brought to the city gates and stoned to death. It says homosexuality is an abomination and punishable by death. It says men can be polygamous and slavery is acceptable. For all I know, that thinking reflected the best wisdom of its time, but it's just plain wrong by any modern standard.[1]

The problem with the Bible, the Qur'an, the Torah – or any sacred text – as an authority is that so much depends on how the text is read and the interests of the reader. The Bible has been used to justify slavery, apartheid, the suppression of women, the 'evils' of sexuality, the 'evils' of homosexuality, a male-only priesthood, the denial of any priests at all, the supremacy of the Pope, the irrelevance of the Pope, the authority of the Church, a denial of the authority of the Church, a feminist agenda, war, pacifism and almost every other position that people may wish to hold.

Postmodernism and hermeneutics have shown that there is no single reading of a text and that much depends on culture, gender and sexuality. There is no 'meta narrative' that will be agreed by everyone, and much depends on the interests of those putting forward a particular interpretation. Translators are almost always, probably necessarily, unfaithful to the original text, so much too will depend on the interests and agendas of the translators. This is a particular issue with translations of the Qur'an: some bodies (and some governments) favour certain translations because these suit their interests, even though many scholars consider them unfaithful to the original text.

The rise of biblical criticism in the West, based initially on the work of the Tübingen school in Germany in the nineteenth century, raised more questions about the authority of the Bible.

---

1 http://webcache.googleusercontent.com/search?q=cache:ymcfHLBoosJ:tv.yahoo.com/the-west-wing/show/episode/2408/

For those who saw the Bible as the unquestioned source of authority, biblical criticism showed that this claim was based on weak foundations. Even within the Catholic Church dissent increased. The First Vatican Council in 1870 affirmed that the Pope, when speaking '*ex cathedra*', could not be in error – but the vote supporting this was taken when various opposing figures returned home, so that their vote could not be recorded. Figures like Loisy and Tyrell rejected aspects of the Church's teaching and took seriously the work done to seek to understand the Bible, its sources and compilation. They were silenced and expelled from the Church, which gave rise to the 'Modernist controversy', culminating in the requirement for all priests to sign the so-called Anti-Modernist Oath in 1910. Anyone aspiring to be a priest who did not sign was not ordained, so for more than 70 years, Catholic priests were forced to accept, on oath, positions that every serious academic knew to be nonsense – for instance, that doctrine does not develop over time or that Divine inspiration does extend to all Scripture so that it is free from error. There is not a single academic biblical scholar who would hold this today, but every Catholic priest had to sign an oath saying that they accepted it. Similarly in 1999, any new Catholic priest (except for Jesuits) had to sign an oath giving 'religious assent of will and intellect to all teachings of the Magisterium'. This has never before been required in the history of the Church, but either priests accept the oath or they cannot be ordained. Many have signed this statement knowing that it is false, but they have had no alternative if they wished to be ordained. Some have been advised to sign but to make a 'mental reservation', although this is hardly an auspicious beginning to priestly ministry.

Religion has, as set out above, often been associated with loyalty to the state and, again, the power of the state has often been used to enforce religious authority. Where loyalty to a particular religious group or perspective is seen as equivalent to, or at least a necessary requirement of, loyalty to the state, it becomes 'reasonable' for state power to be used to ensure orthodoxy. Again what mattered was belonging – and belonging to a given state was often equated with belonging to a particular religion. Great empires have often used religion as a means of maintaining social cohesion. This was certainly the case in the Islamic Empire that arose after the death of the Prophet; it was the case with the Holy Roman Empire based on the authority of Rome; it was the case with the Spanish and Portuguese empires that imposed Catholicism as a means of social control in the territories they conquered; it was the case with the British Empire, the power and influence of the Church of England reaching into every level of government, including seats for leading bishops in the House of Lords. Those who expressed or affirmed opinions that challenged the authority of the state or the religion regarded as normative within a society were seen as not belonging, as outsiders, condemned and often persecuted. Conformity was seen as essential. The legacy of all this has come down to us in the present age in the manner that religions tend to dominate the map of the world depending on where the different colonial powers were active. Thus Islam dominates across North Africa because that was a major area of expansion of the Islamic armies. The Church of England dominates in former British colonies but is almost non-existent elsewhere. Catholicism dominates – or at least is highly influential – where Catholic colonial powers such as France, Spain and Portugal exercised colonial control.

Authority has been used, therefore, by the state to ensure that a single religion is imposed on conquered people, and by religious groups to ensure orthodoxy within their ranks and obedience to the conquering power. Even today dissident voices within religious groups around the world are still silenced. People die for expressing dissent. Authority is a central feature of religion – intended to ensure orthodoxy and to stamp out heresy. While these may seem admirable aims (they maintain the unity of the religious institution and, from a sociological perspective, might make sense), they nevertheless provide no way of differentiating between good and bad religion.

I was having dinner with a prominent Catholic cardinal when some of these issues were discussed. He put the position clearly when he said, 'unity matters more than truth'. The statement shocked me at the time, but I also recognize that from a sociological perspective it has much merit. If unity is not enforced, religion fragments, and once this happens it will not be long before the religion disappears. This can be seen at work within the Anglican Church over the last 50 years. Anglicanism has traditionally been highly tolerant of alternative views. It has prided itself on being a 'broad church', but this breadth has recently been placed under threat because the tolerance has been stretched beyond what some consider acceptable limits. There is no central authority in worldwide Anglicanism, and almost every issue is devolved to local synods. The Anglican bishops meet once every ten years at the Lambeth Conference but they have no binding authority over the constituent Churches of the Anglican Communion. In the case of women priests and bishops, as well as the issue of homosexuality, the Anglican Church is in imminent danger of fragmentation. This is directly related to the lack of any single authority. Each Province of the Anglican Church is effectively independent and can make autonomous decisions. The Archbishop of Canterbury has little authority; there is no 'glue' to hold the Church together. Groups break away and eventually this fragmentation leads to disintegration. It seems entirely possible that the Anglican Church might cease to exist in the next 50 years in anything like its present form, precisely because of this process.

Pragmatically unity does, indeed, matter more than truth, but affirming this is to affirm a cancer at the very heart of religion. Once the centrality of truth is abandoned, something of fundamental human and religious importance is lost. Without a passionate concern for truth, religion becomes dangerous. The Catholic Church itself has, at least partly, recognized this. In an encyclical entitled *Fides et Ratio* (Faith and Reason), Pope John Paul II proclaimed the central importance of philosophy as an independent discipline that was concerned with the search for ultimate truth. What is more, instead of arguing for a single approach to philosophy, the Pope endorsed the importance of its freedom. His main criticism was reserved for the way much modern academic philosophy has lost interest in the great questions of meaning and truth that preoccupied the ancient Greeks: 'How should I live'? 'What really has value'? 'What is the meaning of life'? These questions are central to the human condition and yet, today, are widely ignored. They go to the heart of religion as the basis for personal transformation rather than simply as a way of showing that one belongs to a group. However, the open-minded message of the encyclical, with its emphasis on the autonomy of philosophy, is at variance with a policy from Rome that discourages dissent and, for instance, bans discussion of the possibility of women priests or a moderated stance towards homosexuality. The rhetoric of the encyclical is wonderful; the practice is clearly authoritarian.

The Anglican Lambeth Conference declared in the 1930s that the Anglican Communion is committed to 'an open Bible and a fearless love of truth'. This is a proud banner under which to fly. It means that the biblical text should be available to everyone but that truth is of equal importance. It is a denial of the dining cardinal's principle and an affirmation that truth matters *more* than unity – whatever the sociological costs may be. These, as we have seen, are likely to be great in terms of fragmentation and perhaps even disintegration.

In 1794, Immanuel Kant published *Religion within the Bounds of Reason Alone*, a collection of four essays. These provoked angry responses both from Lutheran authorities, who banned him from writing on religious subjects again on pain of exile (because he challenged accepted religious authorities), but also from other Enlightenment writers, such as Johann Wolfgang von Goethe and Friedrich Schiller (because he still retained a role for religion). The essays threw the crisis into which the Enlightenment had plunged religion into relief. The rise of empiricism made the religious tendency to rely on authority and tradition intellectually unsustainable; scientific discoveries exposed cracks in the foundations of the major faiths. Detailed religious explanations of the origins of the world shifted from being the best available into the realm of quaint antiques, perhaps of sentimental value and anthropological interest but not of much obvious practical use. The cracks in the foundations quickly spread; doubt about one story that had been accepted on the basis of religious authority for generations led to doubt about other stories. Yet as the poet Matthew Arnold later reflected, the place where thinking people were left after the 'sea of faith' had retreated was truly a 'darkling plain'.

As Kant recognized, without religion societies and the individuals who make them up lack a common direction and sense of purpose, lack motivation and hope, not to mention a whole sphere of cultural expression. Yet with religion it seemed they were being held back from exploring the full range of intellectual and technological possibilities by nothing more than superstitions and custom and the need to belong to a community. In simplistic terms, after the Enlightenment people appeared to be divided: the habitual comfort-seekers on the one hand, who accepted authority unquestioningly as part of the price of belonging to a group; the apparently brave, innovative truth-seekers on the other. This was certainly the caricature representation of the relationship between science and religion presented during the twentieth century, and popular writers such as Richard Dawkins still trade on it. He has called faith backward and 'anti-intellectual', has labelled religion as 'the root of all evil' and has suggested that believers are at best misguided fools and at worst sociopaths, all the while portraying atheist scientists as liberal, humane and principled. Thinking people know that the simplistic caricature is not representative. A strictly empiricist, scientific world view is limited and often leads to bigotry, while many people of faith are full of intelligence and integrity and conduct their faith in a state of 'fear and trembling'. Kant attempted to explain how society could aspire to draw on the benefits of religion without sacrificing the coherence or possibilities of an Enlightenment world view.

He sought to develop what the French philosopher August Comte later called a 'religion of humanity' – an organization directing liturgical and ritual practice towards the affirmation of rational principles for the benefit of all mankind. The early sociologists, such as Comte himself, sought to understand the 'function' that religion had within society. They were not interested in questions about the truth of religion. Their only interest – and this is one of the weaknesses of sociology – was in the role or function that religion has within any culture. John Stuart Mill drew on this when he sought to develop a humanistic religion based on altruism as the central principle. Mill wanted people to be committed to the happiness or the good of other human beings, and to be willing to forget themselves. Only by so doing, he argued, might individual happiness be achieved as a by-product of seeking the happiness and well-being of others. Here the main aim is the happiness or well-being of society, which is best achieved, according to Mill, by everyone refusing to seek their own happiness and instead having an unyielding commitment to the happiness of others. Karl Marx was also influenced by sociology, and saw the function of religion in almost entirely negative terms as a control mechanism (though Communists have rarely been shy of borrowing from religion structures and practices useful to achieving their ends).

'Enlightened' models of religion have been proposed by thinkers as diverse as Ludwig Feuerbach, John Stuart Mill, George Eliot and Iris Murdoch, and yet they have never been seriously put into practice because there was never any effective authority behind them and because they simply did not strike a chord with ordinary people. It seems that such a process of rationalization takes away from the power of religion and reduces its effectiveness as a provider of a common direction and purpose, as a motivator and giver of hope. So what future is there for religion and, further, for humanity if religion should be abandoned? The attractions of belonging to a community are very great and are reinforced by the certainty that one's own community is right and others are wrong. In a way this is a conundrum. The power and force of religion derives from its going beyond rational analysis and relying on authoritarian structures, but precisely here lies an apparent failure to be able to differentiate between good and bad religion. Religion that is subject to rational control and evaluation seems to lose its power and appeal, but religion that is outside rational analysis can either be dominated by power and authority or can become highly individualistic. In both cases, religion can sometimes become dangerous.

Habit can be a corrosive force within religion. People settle into patterns of thought and behaviour that they fail to challenge and that harbour lazy short-cuts and thoughtlessness. Authority can then be used to maintain past orthodoxies, even when they have been shown to be outmoded. People in a rut resent being shaken out of it and often become hostile to 'outsiders' or independent thinkers, clinging to outward signs of conformity and pouncing on trivial differences in a way that shows that they are hardly rational, seeking to curtail their own freedom as well as others'. People who are religious by habit often give religion a bad name. Yet habit can be a great strength in religion as well. Monastic and liturgical routines serve to bring the heart and mind back to God and are in themselves a sign of commitment, outward signs of an inward spiritual disposition. They also develop self-discipline and contribute to individuals having control over themselves rather than being dominated by instinct. Virtue ethics, discussed in Chapter 4, involves developing the virtues so that acting well can become a habit. Faith could be seen to encourage habit – at least the sort of faith that develops individuals towards their full potential and seeks to foster compassion, altruism and concern for others.

It seems that habit can have positive and negative aspects, like so much else in religion. In good religion, the aim must be to develop positive habits or virtues that contribute to the good of other human beings. This can be seen in the Aristotelian terms set out in the previous chapter. However, too often authority within religious institutions is concerned to develop habits of obedience, practice and belief that can sometimes have little impact on the individual's development and can foster lack of thought and lack of willingness to challenge authority. People are encouraged to become submissive rather than to question. In bad religion, habit is encouraged, particularly in terms of obedience, because it makes people more co-operative.

Religion is a force for good because it gives people a reason to be good, whether through following laws or making their own more situational decisions. Authority in religious groups maintains cohesion and provides the reward of allowing people to belong to a community and to feel validated, as well as promising a reward after death. This is a powerful mixture and provides a strong incentive for individuals to be compliant, for failure to be so may mean being ostracized from a community and also carries the possibility of exclusion from the promised reward after death. Belief in reward and punishment provides a real incentive to behave well, but it also raises many questions. Could a good and forgiving God really punish for not belonging to a specific community? If not, then what incentive does religion really provide to behave well or to belong to one community rather than another? Who will be rewarded and who punished? How would any just God deal with the moral responsibility of children, psychopaths and the mentally subnormal? These are not easy questions, and yet authority is sometimes afraid of raising them, particularly as whoever controls the keys to life after death has possibly the most powerful weapon of all to ensure control of the believing community. Authority can be a means of suppressing radical questioning and criticizing those who *do* question as being of little faith.

In short, while understandable in terms of seeking to maintain unity, the exercise of authority in religion can also be dangerous. It is too easy for present orthodoxy to be maintained at almost any cost because questioning is frightening and threatening and risks increasing fragmentation. Authority, therefore, that is used to justify lack of independent thought and critical engagement, as well as to encourage a habit of compliance and unquestioning obedience, is often a mark of bad religion and needs to be challenged. This is not to reject all authority but to be aware of its dangers as well as its benefits.

Belonging and unity are important but they cannot be the final word – good religion is about changing people to become better. It is about a call for individual transformation that will result in the transformation of society. Bad religion does not see this and instead emphasizes belonging and uses authority and the rewards it offers to maintain cohesion. Such an approach needs to be resisted and its dangers recognized.

6

The Problem of Texts

The very 'words of God'

Most religions have some core beliefs held in common by all members. Often these originate in, or at least are codified by, a holy text. For Jews, beliefs in one God, in his covenant with the people of Israel and the Law, which he revealed to them through Moses, are all based on the text of the Torah. For Christians, beliefs in Jesus as the Son and Word of God and in the salvation that he offers through repentance, faith and atonement are based on the text of the Bible. For Muslims, beliefs in one God, that Muhammad was the last prophet of God and in the six pillars of faith and five of Muslim practice are based on the Qur'an. Some religions hold that their holy text records the actual words of God, thus that reading it is to receive direct revelation of the truth and doctrines and practices based on these words, which are in direct accordance with the divine will and have absolute authority. This is particularly true of the so-called Abrahamic religions of Judaism, Christianity and Islam, though it may also be said of Sikhism, Mormonism and some other traditions.

A problem arises out of the nature of the written word. Usually the 'words of God' are held to have been received and recorded by one or more religious leaders, and the extent of their influence on the text is always a matter of debate. For instance, one Jewish person may believe that Moses was God's mouthpiece, somehow taken over to transmit the *ipsissima verba* (precise words) of God. Another may believe that Moses was inspired

88

by God to write, but that he communicated the timeless truths revealed to him in terms of language and examples relevant to him and his audience – that his words were in the spirit of what God revealed but not in the literal 'words'. Indeed, one may even doubt that God communicates in words as such – the 'voice' of God 'speaking' may be just a metaphorical way of describing the process of revelation and divine inspiration. If the prophet is more than God's mouthpiece, if he and his context have an influence on shaping the text, there will be debate concerning the text's authority and how it should be interpreted. In the Torah there are many regulations, some of which seem particularly relevant for the early Hebrew community, wandering in the desert – regulations about cleanliness, not eating perishable food liable to be infested with parasites and potentially deadly bacteria, and about being hospitable are some examples. Arguably these regulations are contextual and may not be applicable to later Jewish communities living in different circumstances. But if some regulations and teachings, some 'truths' are not to be taken literally, where does one draw the line?

Even if the role of the prophet is downplayed, there is still room for different interpretations of text. A good illustration of this problem is found in the current Anglican debate over homosexuality. The Anglican tradition encompasses Christians from all over the world and of a wide range of different beliefs. Some are conservative and influenced by the evangelical movement to put the text at the centre of their beliefs and to take it literally. Others are liberal and influenced by academic theology and biblical criticism to see the text in context and as a resource to be interpreted. The current Archbishop of Canterbury, Rowan Williams, is of the latter persuasion and argues that the chief texts cited in discussions about homosexuality have been read out of context and misinterpreted. For instance, like many scholars he sees the story in Genesis 19 — 20 about the destruction of Sodom and Gomorrah as a story about hospitality, written a long time after the events it purports to record in order to make a point to a contemporary readership, not to condemn all homosexual relationships in the twenty-first century. Other Anglican leaders, however, dispute Williams's liberal reading of text and say that this approach undermines the authority of scripture without which the Church will become a rudderless boat. Even if the biblical attitude to homosexuality is unpopular today, if the Bible is true, we cannot pick and choose which bits to accept and which to gloss over.

Taking holy texts 'literally' still demands a level of interpretation. Language, especially when applied to spiritual experiences, is necessarily metaphorical. God is described as walking in the Garden of Eden in the evening and as wrestling with Jacob. Does this mean that God literally has arms, legs and muscles? Translation of holy texts introduces another layer of difficulties. On the one hand, translation makes holy texts and thus divine revelation available to most members of a religion, rendering its truth more widely known and its authority greater; on the other hand, the process of translation is bound to distort the meaning of the text and could thus obscure the truth and mislead people. For instance, the story of the Fall in Genesis 2 — 3 revolves around Eve and then Adam eating an apple. Surely this, it may be argued, is true as it is what it says in the Bible. Actually, in the original Hebrew the word is a general one for 'fruit' and is more commonly applied to a pomegranate. Apples are not common in the Middle East, but neither are pomegranates in England, and translators have traditionally used the word 'apple' to make the story more understandable to the readers of the English editions of the Bible. Eve tempts Adam with a coconut in some translations of the Bible!

It is not just obvious cases like this that can introduce different meanings to a text. When read by Europeans in the Middle Ages, Luke's account of Jesus' birth suggested that Mary must have made a perilous journey to Bethlehem in the snow to give birth in an unheated cow-byre. Christmas cards still show this image. Yet this is the product of people reading-in to the text and is probably far from the truth. Christmas was not celebrated on 25 December until the Church was well established. Nobody knew when Jesus' birthday was – and the presence of shepherds on the hills indicates that it was not winter. Luke says that there was no space in the 'upper room' (Greek: *katalouma*, a private space where honoured guests were usually taken), suggesting that the stable was actually just the ground floor of a typical Middle Eastern caravanserai, where most people lived and slept, not the mean and filthy hut of European imagination. Translation may not just be converting the words of a text from one language to another; it may also be translating a text from being read within its original cultural context to being read within other cultures and other contexts.

In short, because neutral readings of a text are nigh on impossible, it is worth questioning anybody who claims to have literal textual authority for a religious doctrine or practice. 'Good' religion should be open to discussions about the meaning of the text and should neither accept one interpretation without question nor downplay the difficulties inherent in understanding divine revelation through texts. A hallmark of good religion may be the existence of scholars, learned in the original language(s) of the texts, studying and debating their meaning and, further, the presence of good religious education in schools and places of worship, where people are encouraged and enabled to study, discuss and debate texts for themselves. 'Bad' religion may be at work where discussion and debate are stifled and study of the texts reduced to rote learning.

Relativism, fundamentalism and humility

Problems may also arise because while any one religious group may claim that God has spoken authoritatively at various times, this claim cannot be proved to the outside observer and will be rejected by some even within the religious group in question. Assuming that when the claim is made that God has spoken in some way a realist truth claim is being made (see Chapter 2), the possibility of error is always present. This is one of the consequences of realism. Realism maintains that statements are true because they correspond – thus 'God commanded X' is held to be true because God has, indeed, commanded X. However, another consequence of realism is that whatever evidence one has for a claim, the possibility of error exists. A group may indeed believe that 'God commanded X', but it also needs to accept that it is at least possible it might be mistaken. This is extremely important. It means that any supposed religious claim has to be held with a degree of humility. Certainty and humility do not tend to go well together. Most religious believers show little humility in making their claims. Part of the passion and success of religion comes from the certainty with which beliefs are held, and it is this that drives people to be missionaries, to seek to convert others and to dedicate their lives to their religion.

The need for humility is accentuated by other factors. First, any supposed command from God needs interpretation. The context in which it was made needs to be taken into account, as does the precise language in which it was made. Even if it is claimed that God's commands are made outside any context at all (a claim very difficult to defend), hermeneutics as a discipline cannot be ignored. Hermeneutics is now well established and involves interpretation of the written text and the study, among other things, of whether what the writer meant in the original context should decide meaning, or whether the reader's response to the text should be determinative. In Christianity, there has been a considerable emphasis on biblical hermeneutics, but it would be fair to say that the discipline has not yet had any significant impact on Islamic views of textual interpretation of the Qur'an or Hadith. This may, indeed, be the major problem facing Islam as a religion – namely its inability (at least at present) to engage in hermeneutics regarding the Qur'an. Such an engagement is possible at some time in the future, but at present too many Muslims would regard the claim that the Qur'an must be to an extent culturally influenced as simply unacceptable.

Second, whenever a religious imperative is put forward as stemming from God, the possibility of error may occur because whoever interprets the will of God may do so inaccurately. Of course, some religious groups may claim that they are guaranteed to be correct – for instance, because they are inspired by

God. The Catholic Church has traditionally held this view, the Magisterium (the teaching authority in Rome) declaring that it was preserved from error by the grace of God. This culminated in the notion of Papal Infallibility, which was formally adopted as doctrine after the First Vatican Council in 1870. This holds that the Pope, when speaking *ex cathedra*, is infallible on matters of doctrine. In practice the doctrine of infallibility has only been invoked in relation to two pieces of doctrine, that of the Immaculate Conception of Mary (belief in which was made doctrine by Pope Pius IX in 1854) and that of the bodily Assumption of Mary (belief in which was made doctrine by Pope Pius XII in 1950).

The First Vatican Council did acknowledge that doctrine can develop. This was a profound and important acknowledgement; it meant recognizing that Christian ideas about God, Jesus and doctrine in general can and do develop over time; that some earlier ideas may be, at best, less developed than later ones. It also allowed for the possibility that the Church may have been wrong in the past, as it was about Galileo and Copernicus, about slavery, about the implantation of souls at 40 days after conception for males and 90 days for females, about the divine right of kings and many, many other areas. However, once one acknowledges that the church has been wrong in the past, then it logically follows that it may be mistaken today, whether about contraception, women priests, homosexuality or abortion. This step is hard to avoid. Though it does not necessarily mean that the Church *is* mistaken, the possibility of being mistaken exists and cannot be denied. It seems probable to many people that this possibility has been actualized in these cases. To say 'We have made mistakes in the past, but we are guaranteed to be right in everything we teach today' betrays a fundamental flaw in logic – unless some new criterion can be introduced to guarantee present truth claims in a way that is different from previous ones.

This new criterion was the doctrine of infallibility, which allowed for certain Papal pronouncements on doctrine, whether past or future, to be 'ringfenced' and not allowed to be subject to the possibility of error and the questioning that entails.

Religions must, therefore, exercise a degree of humility about the claims they make. However certain they may be, however convinced of their own interpretation, however indubitable it may seem that God has guided them, the possibility of error exists. This is one of the most fundamental ways of distinguishing good from bad religion – whether a religion can recognize at least the possibility of its being in error. It is a major demand because it seems to run counter to most religions, which imply, even if they do not declare, that they could not be wrong. Part of a mature, reflective and deep faith is to recognize the possibility of error.

Even the apostle Paul accepted this possibility when he said that if Jesus was not raised from the dead, Christians would be of all people the most to be pitied. Clearly Paul was convinced that Christianity was ultimately true, but the possibility of error existed. Socrates made the same point when he said that he could not prove the immortality of the soul but was willing to stake his life on this 'if'. He was making a profound point. Socrates was totally convinced of dualism – that a human being is made up of two substances, soul and body, neither of which could be reduced to the other – and that the soul would survive death and have to render an account before the 'judges' for the life that had been lived. However, he also knew that this could not be proved and that the possibility of error existed. He staked everything he had on the immortality of the soul – namely his whole life. He lived every moment in the recognition that he might ultimately have to account for every action and every word and, when he came to die, he knew he had no reason to fear death. Either death was a dreamless sleep or there was an accounting after death, which too held no fear for him. Nevertheless, the fact that he said he was staking his life on an 'if' meant that he recognized the possibility that he could be wrong. Socrates sought to persuade people, to get them to think for themselves, and never to coerce, still less to attempt to force them, to his way of thinking.

Therefore the religious imperatives of any individual religion stem from what are seen to be the commands of God, from some inspired religious leader, from a text or from communal traditions about God. Religions such as Buddhism do not affirm the existence of God in a more conventional sense, the imperative is based on an understanding of ultimate reality and the purpose of life for human beings. However, because the possibility of error is always present, humility is needed.

Many religious believers will not willingly accept this. They may reply by saying:

1. 'We are totally and utterly certain that God has revealed the final truth to us.'
2. 'There is no possibility of our being in error since God has guaranteed the rightness of what God has revealed.'
3. 'The call for me to be humble is, therefore, a call to doubt the unquestioned will of God, which represents a temptation, we should recognize and ignore.'

The key premise here is the second – it is the claim that God in God's self has guaranteed freedom from error. Every human must recognize that certainty cannot be equated with truth. There have been too many examples of people in history being absolutely certain about things that later turned out to be false. That the earth was flat and that slavery was acceptable were both accepted by 'everyone', but everyone today would agree that these views were mistaken. If, of course, the second premise above is right, it is not simply inner certainty that is appealed to but the guarantee of God's revealed will. Problematically, this premise is accepted and endorsed by many religious groups. For instance:

1. The devout Muslim will proclaim this based on the status of the Qur'an. It will be held that it is simply not possible for the Muslim to be wrong about the claim that the Qur'an is God's final and complete revelation. The Qur'an is not simply a document written by a human being based on revelations from God. The Qur'an pre-exists with Allah and is Allah's final and complete revelation of Allah's self and the will of Allah for human beings. Humility is therefore out of place – what is required is obedience.

2. Some evangelical Christians may make a similar claim based on the status of the Bible. In the United States there is a philosophic movement called Reformed Epistemology, which holds that belief in the truth of the Christian message – specifically the message of 'Reformed' Protestant Christianity – and belief in God do not require any justification. The believer has a 'properly ordered noetic structure' – believers see the world correctly because they have been given God's grace to do so. Everyone else has had their reason corrupted by the 'noetic effects of sin'. People have been corrupted, due to the Fall and Original Sin, and have sought to rely on reason alone rather than God's revelation. Only those Christians guided by the grace of God see the world correctly; what is required is obedience to this revelation.[1]

3. Orthodox Jews will see the Torah as being dictated by Moses and representing the word of God to the Jewish community. Faithful obedience to Torah is specifically required, although the rabbis down the ages have been in conversation about precisely how some texts are to be interpreted. Nevertheless, the status of the Torah is simply unquestioned.

In all these cases, talk of humility will be deemed out of place, and it is not surprising that in all three there is an appeal to a written text. It is here that one of the main problems in religion manifests itself. In text-based religions the text itself is supreme and unquestioned. God's will is revealed through the text, and all

---

1 It is important here to make a distinction between Protestant evangelical theology, which sees the final revelation of God as coming from the Bible, and the majority Christian view, which sees Jesus as the Word of God incarnate. By the majority Christian view it is God's Word that brought the world into existence in Genesis, it was God's Word that came to the Jewish prophets and it was God's Word that became incarnate in Jesus. It is the nature of the Word of God that the stories about Jesus in the Bible reveal that is important, not the details of the written text. The revelation of God may therefore be accessed through creation, through history and the individuals who change its direction, as well as through a literal understanding of biblical texts.

that is required is obedience to the text. Any talk of hermeneutics is rejected, and even interpretation of the text will be resisted by many. This is the position the world is in today – many who take a literal view of the text are increasingly drawn towards fundamentalism.

Fundamentalism is on the rise around the world. This is a natural reaction to what is seen as the opposite, namely relativism. The rise of relativism and postmodernism has been marked in the West. The old certainties tend to have died and the emphasis has switched to the importance of perspective. Tolerance has become a new god, proclaimed and insisted on in almost all Western cultures. However, tolerance, unless properly understood, can easily be seen to be the same as relativism, hence the belief that every alternative view is equally acceptable is common. Even the ideas of absolutes such as Truth, Beauty and Justice are undermined and seen by many Western commentators as relativistic notions. This has resulted in Christian certainties also being undermined since many in the West today see Christian claims to truth as simply one more in a set of relativistic claims – no more or less valid than any other.

Any action provokes a reaction, and the rise of relativism in the West has been accompanied by a rise in fundamentalism – in some cases in Christianity but even more so in Islam. Denial of such basic ideas as the claim that there are absolute standards of Justice, Truth and Beauty have led many religions to retreat behind the fortress walls of their own certainties – unwilling to engage with complexity or ambiguity.

Fundamentalism is often closely linked to textual literalism, which is the claim that a particular religious text is divinely inspired and the final source of authority. If this is the case, any attempt to differentiate between good and bad religion will be bound to fail since there is no way to appeal beyond the text. The argument is straightforward:

1. The religious imperative is based – directly or indirectly – on the text.
2. The text is inspired or written by God.

3. There is no appeal beyond the will of God.
4. End of story.

This argument must be resisted, yet this is difficult when appeals to truth must fail and when humility is demanded. Criteria must be established to differentiate between good religion and bad religion, but this is far from straightforward as it runs counter to the central instincts of most religions.

Bad religion can often be a text-based religion. This is not always the case, but texts are dangerous precisely because they can so easily be misused. Because a neutral reading is nigh-on impossible, texts can be held to justify so many different interpretations. Again, the very idea of a text being 'misused' goes to the heart of the argument in this book, namely that some uses of texts may be legitimate but others may not. Bad religion frequently results from an illegitimate use of the text, and almost always occurs where there is a lack of humility about the way the text is read.

The Qur'an

If a neutral reading of any text is impossible; if much depends on the culture in which the text is written and its application to modern issues is a matter of legitimate debate; if the language in which any text is written is problematic (meanings and the use of language can and do change over time); if any text has to be mediated through the mind of the person who wrote it, then complex issues of interpretation arise. Of all these 'ifs', the last one is the most problematic because some will maintain that there is no mediation through a human mind at all. Islam maintains precisely this – the Prophet Muhammad was an empty vessel who, it is held, had no influence whatsoever on the text. The Qur'an was simply dictated to him by the Archangel Gabriel, and Muhammad wrote down the very words of God. (Similar claims are made by some Christians and Jews for their scriptures, although these are more frequently seen as being inspired, rather than literally dictated, by God.) For the devout Muslim this claim may seem persuasive, but even a devout Muslim will have to recognize that alterative views are possible, both within Islam and outside the Muslim community. Even if it is argued that non-Muslims are necessarily in error, almost all Muslims will agree that there are differences of interpretation of the Qur'an among Muslims, particularly when it comes to the texts' application to the modern world. If this is the case, it is unacceptable to argue that one group alone, of all Muslims, has the 'right' interpretation of the Qur'an and every other Muslim's interpretation is wrong.

Why is this claim unacceptable? First, because it allows any group to interpret the Qur'an as it wishes and to declare that it alone has the truth and, therefore, that those who dissent from its interpretation are not true Muslims. There are, and always have been, Muslim groups who hold precisely this position. However, it is refuted within Islam itself, which provides the second reason for rejecting this view. On 27 Ramadan 1425 AH / 9 November 2004 CE, King Abdullah II of Jordan sent the following three questions to 24 of the most senior Muslim religious scholars from all around the world, representing all the branches and schools of Islam:

1. Who is a Muslim?
2. Is it permissible to declare someone an apostate (*takfir*)?
3. Who has the right to undertake issuing *fatwas* (legal rulings)?

Based on the opinions provided by these great scholars (who included the Shaykh Al-Azhar; Ayatollah Sistani, Shaykh Qaradawi and the Grand Mufti of Egypt), in July 2005 the King convened from 50 countries an international Islamic conference of 200 of the world's leading Islamic scholars. The scholars unanimously issued a ruling on three fundamental issues (which became known as the Three Points of the Amman Message):

1. They specifically recognized the validity of all eight Mathhabs (legal schools) of Sunni, Shia and Ibadhi Islam; of

traditional Islamic theology (Ash'arism); of Islamic mysticism (Sufism); and of true Salafi thought – and came to a precise definition of who is a Muslim.

2. Based upon this definition they forbade *takfir* (declarations of apostasy) between Muslims.

3. Based upon the Mathahib they set forth preconditions for the issuing of legal rulings, thereby exposing illegitimate edicts in the name of Islam.

The Three Points were unanimously adopted by the Islamic world's political and temporal leaderships at the Organization of the Islamic Conference summit at Mecca in December 2005. They were also adopted by six other international Islamic scholarly assemblies, culminating in the International Islamic Fiqh Academy of Jeddah in July 2006. In total, over 500 leading Muslim scholars worldwide unanimously endorsed the Amman Message and its Three Points.

This amounts to a historical, universal and unanimous religious and political consensus (*ijmā'*) of the Ummah (community) of Islam, as well as a consolidation of traditional, orthodox Islam.

The significance of this is:

1. That it is the first time in over a thousand years that the Ummah has formally and specifically come to such a pluralistic mutual inter-recognition; and

2. That such a recognition is religiously legally binding on Muslims since the Prophet said: 'My Ummah will not agree upon an error.'[2]

The Amman Message provides a basis for unity and a resolution to disputes between Muslims. In addition, for non-Muslims, it safeguards the legal methodologies of Islam (the Mathahib) and preserves traditional Islam's internal 'checks and balances'. It thus assures balanced Islamic solutions for essential issues such as human rights; women's rights; freedom of religion; legitimate

---

2 Ibn Majah, Sunan, Kitab al-Fitan, Hadith 4085.

jihad; good citizenship of Muslims in non-Muslim countries; and just and democratic government. It also exposes the illegitimate opinions of radical fundamentalists and terrorists from the point of view of true Islam.

This is of profound importance, for it represents the agreed view of all the main Muslim groups throughout the world (who often do not agree on significant issues) and precisely prevents any one group claiming that 'We alone have the truth and all others are wrong' or, to put this in the context of this chapter, to say 'We alone have the correct interpretation of the Qur'an and all others are wrong.' No similar meeting of worldwide Christians or Jews has taken place or is, indeed, likely to take place. The Amman Message is significant primarily because it appeals to a very broad consensus, acknowledges differences but also shows an attitude of humility and a willingness to listen to alternative perspectives, albeit from within Islam.

The Amman Message says that:

Islam rejects extremism, radicalism and fanaticism – just as all noble, heavenly religions reject them – considering them as recalcitrant ways and forms of injustice. Furthermore, it is not a trait that characterizes a particular nation; it is an aberration that has been experienced by all nations, races, and religions. They are not particular to one people; truly they are a phenomenon that every people, every race and every religion has known.

(Incidentally, as we shall see below, this provides an important starting point for a demarcation between good and bad religion.) The Message goes on to say that:

[w]e denounce and condemn extremism, radicalism and fanaticism today, just as our forefathers tirelessly denounced and opposed them throughout Islamic history. They are the ones who affirmed, as do we, the firm and unshakeable understanding that Islam is a religion of [noble] character traits in both its ends and means; a religion that strives for the good of the

people, their happiness in this life and the next; and a religion that can only be defended in ways that are ethical; and the ends do not justify the means in this religion.[3]

Each group within Islam still maintains its own distinctiveness, each group still puts forward its own interpretation of the Qur'an and has its own view of history (for instance, the major split between Sunni and Shiite Islam is due to different accounts of history in the decades following the Prophet's death), but each group also recognizes that other groups are also faithful Muslims and commits itself to refraining from condemnation. It was an extraordinary and important step. As George Yeo, the foreign minister of Singapore, declared in the 60th Session of the United Nations General Assembly in 2005 (about the Amman Message), 'Without this clarification, the war against terrorism would be much harder to fight.'

Since then Islam has gone further by issuing in Autumn 2007 an open letter to major Christian leaders signed by more than 130 Muslim scholars and leaders called 'A Common Word between Us and You'. The letter was sent to Pope Benedict, the Archbishop of Canterbury, the heads of the Lutheran, Methodist and Baptist Churches and the Orthodox Patriarchs among others. It identifies the principles of accepting only one God and living in peace as common ground between Christianity and Islam. It insists that Christians and Muslims worship the same God. It compares passages in the Qur'an and the Bible, concluding that both emphasize 'the primacy of total love and devotion to God' and the 'love of the neighbour. As Muslims, we say to Christians that we are not against them and that Islam is not against them – so long as they do not wage war against Muslims on account of their religion, oppress them and drive them out of their homes.' The letter adds:

To those who nevertheless relish conflict and destruction for their own sake or reckon that ultimately they stand to gain

---

3 See http://ammanmessage.com/index.php?option=com_content&task=view&id=16&Itemid=30&limit=1&limitstart=1.

through them, we say our very eternal souls are all also at stake if we fail to sincerely make every effort to make peace and come together in harmony.[4]

'A Common Word between Us and You' is a document of immense significance. It was rarely possible to use the word 'Islam' to stand for a single view before this letter. One of the signatories, Dr Aref Ali Nayed, a senior adviser at the Cambridge Inter-Faith Programme, told the BBC that the document should be seen as a landmark. 'There are Sunnis, Shias, Ibadis and even the . . . Ismailian and Jaafari schools, so it's a consensus', he said. Professor David Ford, director of the Cambridge Inter-Faith Programme, said the letter was unprecedented: 'If sufficient people and groups heed this statement and act on it, then the atmosphere will be changed into one in which violent extremists cannot flourish.'[5] The letter was signed by prominent Muslim leaders, politicians and academics, including the Grand Muftis of Bosnia and Herzegovina, Russia, Croatia, Kosovo and Syria, the Secretary-General of the Organization of the Islamic Conference, the former Grand Mufti of Egypt and the founder of the Ulema Organization in Iraq. It therefore represents a united view from across the Muslim community – a united view that would, perhaps, not be possible from Christians or Jews as a whole.

The Amman Message and the open letter not only represent a remarkable degree of unity across Islam but also provide good grounds for differentiating between good and bad religion. These documents represent the moderate, articulate, balanced and rational view of Islam and reject the simplicity of, for instance, any single reading of Qur'anic Surahs in the way beloved of the literalists.

It seems that a mark of good religion may be an awareness of the competing poles of relativism and fundamentalism and the aim to stand between the two, resisting the crude literalism and

---

4 See http://www.acommonword.com/index.php?lang=en&page=option1.
5 See http://www.interfaith.cam.ac.uk/en/resources/papers/professor-david-ford-response-to-a-common-word?searched=common+word&advsearch=oneword&highlight=ajaxSearch_highlight+ ajaxSearch_highlight1+ajaxSearch_highlight2.

authoritarian oppression that go hand in hand with fundamentalism but also resisting the denial of truth, meaning and values that go hand in hand with relativism. Participation in ecumenical discussions, in regular attempts to build bridges between branches of the religion that have diverged, and in attempts to achieve agreement over points of belief and practice may all be positive signs of good religion at work.

7

Science and Religion

The relationship between science and religion has not always been a happy one. Traditionally religion has claimed to provide a comprehensive picture of the universe that it held to be true. It claimed to be able to explain everything, including movements of the heavenly bodies, the cycles of the seasons, fertility of animals, crops and humans, the weather, success in battle as well as love, sin and evil. It also held the keys to life after death. Religion provided a total picture of reality, reinforced by priests and the universities that existed all endorsing the same picture. In this stable world, science came as an unwelcome intruder. It offered a new paradigm of truth – free from the traditions of the past, from the authority of religious organizations and sacred texts. It did not depend on revelation and appealed to only one standard, that of empirical evidence. What was more; this new understanding could be widely understood and demonstrated to all who were interested. Tradition and authority were no longer enough: people wanted proof, and science could provide it. Science worked, it succeeded. Its explanations bore fruit and changed people's lives in radical ways.

The reaction of many religions to science has initially been negative. By claiming an autonomy and authority of its own, science struck a blow at the heart of the religious understanding of reality. Once some corners of the religious picture began to unravel it was not a matter of making small adjustments – rather the whole basis of religious authority was challenged. Not only were sacred scripture and the authority of religious hierarchies undermined but, more seriously, the whole way in which religion looked at the world was thrown into question. The most commonly quoted example is, of course, the discovery by Copernicus and then Galileo that the earth went round the sun rather than the earth being stationary as sacred scripture claimed. The earth was not 'fixed and immoveable', the stars did not rotate round the earth in concentric spheres, as Aristotle had held. This was a revolutionary idea and it turned round the whole way in which humans thought of themselves. Instead of God having created the earth and humans being the centre of the universe and the pinnacle of God's creation, as the Bible and the Church taught, the earth was now seen as an average-sized planet rotating around an ordinary star. The supposed final authority of the Church was shown to be flawed. Its claims, undisputed for centuries, were now shown to be fallible. The priests and university professors who supported them were mistaken. Doubt crept in. If religion could be wrong about such a basic matter, what else could it be wrong about? If the authority of the Bible and the Church was no longer undoubted, maybe all religious claims could be questioned.

The claim to hold all truth, which many religions have and sometimes still do claim, is vulnerable: once one truth claim is shown to be false then, logically, others may be considered false as well. Doubt is insidious. It spreads and undermines certainty. René Descartes, the French philosopher, embarked on methodological doubt – the attempt to doubt everything and to start anew based on firm foundations. David Hume, more devastatingly, introduced scepticism into the West and argued that only those things could be known that came to human beings from the five senses, and even these could not be trusted. A ship that went through the water did not necessarily create the wake – even cause and effect could be doubted. However, Descartes and Hume did not discover philosophical scepticism – it has had a long history. One of the most influential figures was the Muslim philosopher, Al-Ghazali.

Al-Ghazali was born in 1058 CE in what is now western Iran. He studied Islamic Law and so impressed the vizier to the Seljuk Sultans that he appointed him as a professor in a Baghdad University in 1091 CE. However, in 1095 he went through a spiritual crisis. He resigned his position, saying that he was going to Mecca on pilgrimage, but in fact disposed of all his wealth and became a poor Sufi. He travelled to Damascus, Jerusalem, Medina and then to Mecca, and in 1096 went almost into seclusion (apart from one short lecturing period). He died in 1111. Al-Ghazali came to think that Greek philosophy and Neoplatonism had been used to distort the teachings of Islam. He realized, however, that he could not claim this until he himself became an expert in philosophy and could understand its ideas thoroughly – so he spent the next three years studying philosophy, and then wrote *The Intentions of the Philosophers*. This was a masterly summary of Greek philosophical thought, particularly of Plato, and showed a deep understanding and apparent sympathy, but for Al-Ghazali this was but a prelude to his main work. His central book was entitled *The Incoherence of the Philosophers*, and represented a sustained and devastating attack on philosophy and the use of Aristotle by Islamic thinkers. Al-Ghazali discovered philosophical scepticism, which would not be commonly seen in the West until Descartes. He argued that the senses could not be trusted: for instance, human beings look at a shadow and think it does not move, but realize this is mistaken; we look at the sun and think it is as small as a coin, but astronomy tells us it is bigger than our earth. If our sense experience is vulnerable, perhaps what are regarded as propositions that are held to be true based on reason are not to be trusted either. Reason has shown that our sense experience can be fallible. It follows that perhaps there is a higher authority that would show that our reason cannot be trusted either. This is scepticism of our reason. Al-Ghazali's conclusion was that if both reason and the senses are not to be trusted, the only way forward is to trust God. This led him to a negative view of science and philosophy if they in any way contradicted the text of the Qur'an, which he took to have been directly revealed by God and therefore more reliable as a guide to truth than science.

In the West it took centuries for doubt to spread, but as science in the West advanced with the Enlightenment, it explained more and more and achieved continually greater understanding of the natural world. For the early scientists, science revealed yet more clearly the glory and wonder of God's creation. Many of the earliest astronomers were Jesuits, and most early scientists were also deeply religious; but as the explanations provided by science became more comprehensive, so the need for religion began to recede. Religion, while still important, increasingly came to be seen by some as peripheral. Darwin showed that human beings had evolved, through natural selection, from other animals. Species were not fixed as the Genesis story of Adam and Eve seemed to imply. Adaptation was everywhere. Ludwig Feuerbach and early sociologists such as Auguste Comte saw humans as essentially material beings and religions as products of human need that fulfilled various important functions within society but did not contain independent truth. Marx analysed religion in terms of power structures within society and saw religion as on the side of the strong and powerful and as one of the means used to keep working people in what was effectively slavery to the property-owning classes. Emancipation could come from the rejection of religion and authority, which would open the door to a new social order. Freud dismissed religion as a neurosis and an illusion fostered in early childhood.

In comparison with the increasingly comprehensive scientific picture of the world, religion seemed to become ever more irrelevant or a part-time hobby for those who were so inclined. Little seemed to remain of its claim to truth. A scientific picture of reality seemed to have won the day, and religion, at least in the West, was in decline. This was well expressed in Matthew Arnold's poem 'Dover Beach'

> The sea is calm to-night.
> The tide is full, the moon lies fair
> Upon the straits;—on the French coast, the light
> Gleams and is gone; the cliffs of England stand,
> Glimmering and vast, out in the tranquil bay.
> Come to the window, sweet is the night-air!
> Only, from the long line of spray
> Where the sea meets the moon-blanched land,

Listen! you hear the grating roar
Of pebbles which the waves draw back, and fling,
At their return, up the high strand,
Begin, and cease, and then again begin,
With tremulous cadence slow, and bring
The eternal note of sadness in.

Sophocles long ago
Heard it on the Aegean, and it brought
Into his mind the turbid ebb and flow
Of human misery; we
Find also in the sound a thought,
Hearing it by this distant northern sea.

The Sea of Faith
Was once, too, at the full, and round earth's shore
Lay like the folds of a bright girdle furled.
But now I only hear
Its melancholy, long, withdrawing roar,
Retreating, to the breath
Of the night-wind, down the vast edges drear
And naked shingles of the world.

Ah, love, let us be true
To one another! for the world, which seems
To lie before us like a land of dreams,
So various, so beautiful, so new,
Hath really neither joy, nor love, nor light,
Nor certitude, nor peace, nor help for pain;
And we are here as on a darkling plain
Swept with confused alarms of struggle and flight,
Where ignorant armies clash by night.[1]

---

1 Matthew Arnold, 'Dover Beach', in Helen Gardner (ed.), *The New Oxford Book of English Verse*, Oxford: Oxford University Press, 1972, p. 703.

The 'Sea of Faith' did indeed once circle the world, but science increasingly challenged and undermined it in the West. Instead of whole communities seeing religion as the central part of their identity, religion was effectively privatized. Western societies bought into the scientific world view wholesale. Scientists were the new authority figures, taking over from the priests of previous generations. Increasingly, human beings were accepted to be complex animals, motivated by the base desires to live and reproduce, mortal and fallible, only capable of leaving a material legacy after death. Religion and the hope it brought became something not talked about in polite society. Increasingly it was seen as a hobby, a personal interest or eccentricity – harmless provided it did not infringe on the public sphere. This was linked with human beings becoming disconnected from the natural world, and with the process of industrialization. People's lives became increasingly busy; they had little time to reflect. Medical discoveries made it unnecessary for most people to consider the prospect of death until old age. Religious and existential questions became peripheral; the real business of life was focused on the here and now, improving one's material wealth and social standing. One could manage in life, pay the mortgage, bring up children and watch sport without considering religion at all.

In Islam the attitude to science varied. It was often seen as a threat because of the status of the Qur'an as the very word of God, a stance exemplified by Al-Ghazali. Science, after the enormous Islamic renaissance up to the thirteenth century CE, went into decline in Islam because it was seen by many to pose a threat to religion.

From the nineteenth century onwards, by contrast, Christians in the West developed hermeneutics and biblical criticism, and came to see the Bible as a book written by humans, even if the writers were inspired by God. There were, of course, many who resisted this approach – in the Catholic Church, as we have seen (p. 80), the 'Modernist' controversy resulted in the 'Anti-Modernist Oath', which all Catholic priests had to swear from 1910 and which rejected biblical criticism and the new challenges to the authority of the Church. There was also a rise in more fundamentalist Protestant sects that, particularly in the United States, held on to the Bible as the literal word of God.

Most Christians today make no claims to biblical inerrancy and are quite happy to see, for instance, the Genesis account of the creation of the world as a myth that conveys deep underlying truths about the dependence of the world on God, but not as a literal account. Islam finds such an approach far more difficult due to the claimed status of the Qur'an. It has yet to apply hermeneutics to the Qur'an or to see it is as a document that may be culturally embedded and culturally dependent. The relation between science and religion is important here: if any of the Qur'an's Surahs can be shown by science to be wrong, the whole status of the Qur'an comes under threat. Many Muslims seek to show that the Qur'an is fully compatible with science and, indeed, that it anticipated modern scientific discoveries – for instance by describing the development of the embryo in a way, it is claimed, that could not have been known at the time (although non-Muslims will see a remarkable congruence between the Qur'an's understanding of the developing embryo and that of the Greek physician, Galen). Other Muslim thinkers, however, saw science as a threat and treated science with suspicion as a Western import that challenged faith.

The relation between science and religion goes to the heart of the debate about good and bad religion. Science and religion are both interested in truth, but there cannot be two truths. While the most obvious way to respond is to suggest that one must be in error, it could also be that science is true and that religion is true, and therefore their truths must be compatible.

This second option was developed by the Muslim thinker Ibn Rushd (known as Averroës in the West). Ibn Rushd argued that the Qur'an and Shariah Law cannot be understood without using philosophy and science. Only those trained in philosophy will be able to arrive at an accurate understanding of the text, and they need to teach those who do not have this understanding. He was, therefore, an elitist who believed that a superficial understanding of both the Qur'an and Shariah Law would be misleading and false. He was a strong critic of most of the different schools of ideas in Islam in his day.

Part of Ibn Rushd's appeal was his meticulous attention to detail. He wrote three commentaries on Aristotle: the short, the middle and the long. Sometimes there are three levels of commentary on a single Aristotelian text. The long commentaries offer line-by-line analysis of Aristotle. Ibn Rushd realized that there was a tension between philosophy and the text of the Qur'an, and it made him nervous. He told one of his students how an older philosopher, Ibn Tufayl, who also happened to be the caliph's medical adviser, introduced him to the caliph. Ibn Rushd was about 42 at the time, and he described the episode like this:

> When I entered into the presence of the Prince of the Believers, Ab'u Yaq'ub, I found him with Ab'u Bakr Ibn Tufayl alone. Ab'u Bakr began praising me, mentioning my family and ancestors and generously including in the recital things beyond my real merits. The first thing that the Prince of the Believers said to me, after asking me my name, my father's name and my genealogy was: 'What is their opinion about the heavens?' – referring to the philosophers – 'Are they eternal or created?' Confusion and fear took hold of me, and I began making excuses and denying that I had ever concerned myself with philosophic learning; for I did not know what Ibn Tufayl had told him on the subject. But the Prince of the Believers understood my fear and confusion, and turning to Ibn Tufayl began talking about the question of which he had asked me, mentioning what Aristotle, Plato and all the philosophers had said, and bringing in besides the objections of the Muslim thinkers against them.[2]

Experts in Islamic Law were (and are) divided into several schools of thought, among them the M'alikite school. The M'alikites, together with the Hanbalites, were called 'the people of Tradition'. Their founder, M'alik b. Anas, is perhaps best known for what he

---

2 See http://www.muslimphilosophy.com/hmp/chp28.doc.

said when asked about Qur'anic references to God sitting on his throne. Prominent Muslim theologians took this language to be an allegorical way of expressing God's majesty, but not M'alik, who replied: 'The sitting is known; its modality is unknown. Belief in it is an obligation and raising questions regarding it is a heresy.' The M'alikites had no use for philosophy or science in matters of religious doctrine, although they did allow for argument on some points of religious law – something that Ibn Rushd used to make his case for philosophy and science. Ibn Rushd was to provide a strong argument against Al-Ghazali's scepticism in a book called *The Incoherence of the Incoherence* (directed, of course, at Al-Ghazali's *The Incoherence of the Philosophers*). However, because this challenged a literal reading of the Qur'an he was driven from his post and his home town of Córdoba and became a refugee. Ibn Rushd had always loved to preach in the mosque, and one of his early biographers preserves these words:

> The worst thing that happened to me in my afflictions was when I and my son, Abdallāh entered a mosque in Córdoba at the time of the evening prayer, and some of the lowest of the common people made a commotion against us and ejected us from it.[3]

He was placed on trial, his books were burned and two or three years later he was exiled to Lucena, a small Jewish town south of Córdoba.

The legacy of Ibn Rushd has been enormous. In a book entitled *The Decisive Treatise* he discusses philosophy and science in legal terms. He questions whether scientific and philosophic study is obligatory or recommended. Ibn Rushd draws on the four sources of Islamic Law: the Qur'an, the Hadith, the consensus of the Muslim community and analogical reasoning, which was the sort of reasoning used by those lawyers who allowed for argumentation when interpreting the Qur'an. He argued that a craftsman is known by his works and science studies the works

---

3 http://www.aristotle-aquinas.org/peripatetikos-6/DecisiveTreatiseAverroes.pdf.

God, who is the divine Craftsman. Islamic Law, he argued, urges Muslims to do precisely this: to study the heavens and the earth. Muslims should use reason to study the natural world as the handiwork of God.

Ibn Rushd replied to critics who questioned why a faithful Muslim should use Aristotle and Greek philosophers who were not Muslims as follows:

> . . . whenever we find in the works of our predecessors of former nations a theory about beings and a reflection on them conforming to what the conditions of demonstration require, we ought to study what they said about the matter and what they affirmed in their books. And we should accept from them gladly and gratefully whatever in these books accords with the truth, and draw attention to and warn against what does not accord with the truth . . .[4]

Trained scientists are needed. Ibn Rushd recognizes that, in ignorant hands, philosophy and science can lead people astray, which is why trained Islamic thinkers are required:

> We can say that a man who prevents a qualified person from studying books of philosophy, because some of the most vicious people may be thought to have gone astray through their study of them, is like a man who prevents a thirsty person from drinking cool, fresh water until he dies of thirst, because some people have choked to death on it.[5]

Ibn Rushd maintains that Islam is true and that it leads people to the happiness of knowing God and God's creation, but that different persons are led differently. Some have a temperament and nature that fit them for following science and philosophic logic and, therefore, for such persons real faith will be deeper if

---

4 *Decisive Treatise*, cap. 1, p. 48. All quotations from Ibn Rushd's *Decisive Treatise* are from George Hourani's translation (London: Luzac, 1976).

5 *Decisive Treatise*, cap. 1, p. 49.

rational methods are followed. Firm assent to faith comes from whichever sort of argument a person can grasp. It follows that assent to Islam is open to everyone except the stubborn and the negligent. That, says Ibn Rushd, is what the Qur'an means when it says '[s]ummon to the way of your Lord by wisdom and by good preaching, and debate with them in the most effective manner'.[6] 'Wisdom' is philosophy and science, and 'preaching' is a rhetorical exercise, while 'debate' is dialectical. All of this brings Ibn Rushd to a most important point: since Islam is true and urges rational enquiry, science and philosophy do not lead to conclusions that contradict Islam, for – in Ibn Rushd's own words – 'truth does not oppose truth but accords with it and bears witness to it'.[7] Ibn Rushd discusses this problem in detail. Reason and the Qur'an both seek truth and therefore cannot contradict each other. If reason (philosophy) reveals something that the Qur'an does not mention, there is no tension. If reason and the text of the Qur'an are contradictory, the text needs to be interpreted allegorically. Contradictions can only arise when philosophy and the text really do contradict each other. Ibn Rushd says that this cannot happen because truth does not oppose truth.

He argues that his position is supported by the Qur'an, which admits to ambiguity within the text in this famous verse:

> He it is who has sent down to you the Book, containing certain verses clear and definite – they are the essence of the Book – and others ambiguous. Now those in whose hearts is mischief go after the ambiguous passages, seeking discord and seeking to interpret them allegorically. But no one knows their interpretation except God and those who are well grounded in science. (3.7)

Different Muslim scholars will, however, interpret this text differently. The Qur'an addresses different sorts of readers. It has

---

6 16.125, quoted in *Decisive Treatise*, cap. 1, p. 49.
7 *Decisive Treatise*, cap. 2, p. 50.

an apparent as well as an inner meaning because some readers cannot understand anything beyond the apparent meaning. To quote Ibn Rushd:

> God has been gracious to those of His servants who have no access to demonstration, on account of their natures, habits or lack of facilities for education: He has coined for them images and likenesses of these things, and summoned them to assent to those images . . .[8]

The Qur'an also nurtures the learned and so, besides images, it has verses that are seemingly contradictory because they '. . . draw the attention of those who are well grounded in science to the interpretation which reconciles them'.[9] Each reader will therefore approach the text based on his or her level of understanding, and the Qur'an can speak to different individuals at different levels. If the Qur'an is understood as addressing each person according to his or her ability, different readers must be treated differently. Ibn Rushd mentions evidence that even the earliest Muslims differentiated between the apparent and the inner meaning of the Qur'an. The inner meaning should not be communicated to those who are incapable of understanding it. In the words of the fourth caliph, cited by Ibn Rushd: 'Speak to people about what they know. Do you want God and His Prophet to be accused of lying?'[10]

Ibn Rushd's essential argument is that to reject reason and science in the interests of defending religion is a grave mistake. If religion is right and science wrong, the wrongness of science needs to be demonstrated, which seems very hard to do. It may be maintained that a scientific account of reality is incomplete or

---

8 *Decisive Treatise*, cap. 2, p. 59.
9 *Decisive Treatise*, cap. 2, p. 51.
10 Much of this material on Ibn Rushd comes from an excellent article, 'A Muslim Perspective on Philosophy and Religion: The Decisive Treatise of Averroës', by Thérèse Bonin, Duquesne University, Pittsburgh, to whom grateful acknowledgement is made. The whole article can be found at http://www.aristotle-aquinas.org/peripatetikos-6/.

inadequate, but to say that it is simply wrong is a difficult under-taking. Bad religion fears science – it fears that its own claims to truth will be challenged and undermined and so will react negatively to science. It will refuse thought and employ rhetoric. It will not engage on a level playing field with science by, for in-stance, seeking to deny, perhaps, any congruity between science and religion. Fear is dangerous, and when religious people and institutions are fearful they tend to retreat behind the fortress walls of their own certainties. In particular, they tend to rely on authority, whether this is from tradition, a sacred text or an institution. Doubt and questioning are condemned and faith is made to require the subservience of reason. Ibn Rushd stands in a long and proud tradition of good religion that is not afraid of science but embraces it.

Today, major religious figures embrace both science and reli-gion and see no incompatibility at all between them. Academics such as Keith Ward, John Polkinghorne, Paul Davies and many others argue that the revelations of science require God and that, without God, the scientific understanding of reality is in-complete. They see sacred scripture and the tradition of religion as complementing and fulfilling scientific understanding rather than competing with it. Of course, this means that not all bibli-cal texts can be taken literally, but most Christian theologians have long accepted this. There is no contradiction, therefore, be-tween the Hebrew and Christian scriptures and modern science, provided the former are read allegorically or as myths conveying deeply embedded truths. Effectively this was the position taken by Ibn Rushd.

This certainly does not mean that 'science has won' and that religion is subservient to science. Quite the reverse is the case. Religion often challenges science by showing that its understand-ing of reality is partial and inadequate. Questions of meaning, purpose, morality, aesthetics, human relationships and life after death are not addressed by science. As Galileo is reputed to have put it, 'Religion teaches how to get to heaven, not how the heav-ens go'. Good religion should complement science whereas bad religion goes against it. Good religion provides insights into the human condition that are not available elsewhere, it provides a different way of looking at the universe and, possibly most important, it sees the universe as full of meaning and purpose.

Reference has already been made to Immanuel Kant's fundamental claim that the universe is rational. This is also a claim made by science – the universe can be understood using reason. In a sense this is a faith claim made by all scientists. We live in a universe that can be understood, and science makes a major contribution towards developing this understanding. Religion, however, goes further and sees meaning and purpose behind the universe. This is something some scientists, such as Richard Dawkins, deny, but by no means all do so. Dawkins famously says that there are only 'how' questions and no 'why' questions. Almost all religions argue that this is mistaken – purpose and meaning interpenetrate every aspect of the universe.

We now know that the universe is far more complex than was ever conceived possible in the past. Our understanding of reality is partial and limited. Human language and concepts are very good at dealing with middle-sized objects but not at engaging with the very large (galaxies and the universe as a whole) or the very small (the world of nanotechnology and, at the Planck scale, the quantum world). At the Planck scale 'material reality' ceases to exist – there are simply waves of pure potentiality. These waves of potentiality are acted on by consciousness. It is impossible to observe an event at the quantum level without changing it. Science has long assumed that material reality is the ultimate, and scientists such as Isaac Newton sought to explain how this material reality operates and the laws by which it is governed. We now know that to talk of 'material reality' is a mistake. Material reality is simply reality as we perceive it – it is the way in which waves of pure potentiality have come together. What governs these waves of potentiality and how they function are issues that science and theology both debate.

The very understanding of God may need to change in the future, and good religion is open to this. In the earliest days the gods were found in the woods and trees and particularly at crossing points. Then the gods were seen as dwelling in the mountains or the sky, although they were highly anthropomorphic and had petty lusts and jealousies (the Greek, Roman and Norse gods are good examples). The Prophet Muhammad stood out against these cultural images of his time and overthrew the idols in Mecca and the petty gods worshipped by the tribes of the Arabian Peninsula. He was in the tradition of the *hannif* – a worshipper of a single God, of whom Abraham was the forerunner. As philosophy developed, God came to be seen as single ('wholly simple') and was beyond time and space – albeit still conceived in personal terms. These understandings of the divine were all limited by the knowledge of their time. Science forces religion to re-evaluate its understanding of the divine and the interaction of the heavenly and earthly worlds. This re-evaluation should not be threatening to religion – it is a mark of the development of human understanding that is positive and important.

God or ultimate reality has always been a mystery beyond the capacity of the human mind to conceptualize, but that does not mean there cannot be better, though still inadequate, ways of trying. God can no longer be thought of as an old man with a white beard occasionally intervening in the world. New understandings and approaches are needed and science can help with these. This does not undermine revelation or sacred texts, but it does emphasize that revelation can only be made within the capacities to understand of those to whom things are revealed. To try to explain to Neolithic people the nature of quantum reality would be folly in the extreme – the most one could attempt would be to try to convey some very limited view of the nature of quantum reality, but this would, inevitably, be partial and inaccurate. The same applies to the divine, which lies beyond the power of human comprehension.

Paul wrote, 'When I was a child, I spoke as a child, but now I am a man I have put away childish things' (1 Cor. 13.11). Childish understandings of God and religion need to be abandoned and a more mature and deep understanding of religious reality embraced. Ibn Rushd was right – religion speaks to different people at different levels. The simple person who worships in the synagogue, mosque, gurdwara, mandir, church or chapel engages with God at one level, the philosopher, theologian and scientist at another. But one level is not necessarily 'better' than another. Faith is not about understanding – it involves changing one's life and orienting oneself towards that which is good, beautiful, significant and enduring in the universe, which is encapsulated by the word God. It will involve sacrifice and certainly commitment, and will demand a complete change in priority and perspective. Increased understanding of God does not make the faith journey any easier nor the demands of living a life of faith any the less.

The fact that science can challenge and illuminate reality does not in any way need to diminish the power or mystery of religion, just as religion does not diminish the importance of science. Sacraments, rituals and mysteries point beyond themselves to an unseen world and reality that human beings can only dimly comprehend. But the power of worship and the reality towards which religion points are not diminished but enhanced by science. The universe is far more glorious and extraordinary than the finest poets or painters could ever have imagined. Good religion helps human beings to recognize this and also to engage in the 'deep magic' (as C. S. Lewis famously put it) or Holy Mystery (Karl Rahner) of meaning and purpose that lies at the heart of reality.

8

Justice

Benjamin Disraeli once defined justice as 'truth in action'. Justice is an integral part of religion, and one of the central tenets of all religions is that justice must be done. Religions claim to bring justice, providing laws, rules and an authority. Justice is seen to underpin the well-being of society. The gods or God are seen to want justice above everything else. A society with religion and the justice it brings is 'better off' than it would have been without. Yet just as the truths religions claim are different, so are their concepts of and methods of administering justice.

Concepts of justice

In Christianity and the Hebrew Scriptures, a lack of justice is equated with sin. To bring justice and peace is seen to be the aim of war, and justice is linked with God's will and God's kingdom. King David, the greatest of Israel's kings, is praised because he executed justice (2 Sam. 8.15). In the book of Job, one of Job's comforters, who come to him in his distress, says that God does not pervert justice or judgement (Job 8.3) and is known for the excellence of God's justice (Job 37.23). Proverbs 21.3 says that to do justice and judgement is more acceptable to God than sacrifice. Isaiah 9.7 and 56.1 both say that God will establish God's kingdom with justice and judgement. In the book of Amos, justice is seen as the highest priority and God says that God is uninterested in and will not listen to hymns and songs but wants justice to flow like a river. In Jeremiah 20.3 and 50.7 God's kingdom is described as the habitation of justice. There is no more powerful theme running through the Hebrew Scriptures than the importance of justice.

In Islam, justice is one of the highest values that every Muslim is called on to practise, and all Islamic societies are meant to be established on the principles of justice. God wants to see justice done more than anything else. The Prophet Muhammad was very clear on the demands made on those who execute justice, and that such justice must always be carried out fairly, honestly, truthfully and free of self-interest. In the Qur'an, Surah 3.18 records God maintaining God's creation with justice; 3.21 commands the slaying of those who act unjustly; 3.108 maintains that God does not desire injustice to any of God's creatures. In 4.40 God is said not to do injustice 'even to the weight of an atom'. God is said to enjoin justice (7.29) and to reward and punish with justice (10.4). The Qur'an is quite specific that God does not do any injustice to men, but men are unjust to themselves (10.44) – God wants justice above all else and all Muslims are exhorted to practise justice in every aspect of their lives. Those who are unjust will receive everlasting chastisement, and even if they owned the whole of the earth and offered this in compensation, it would not be enough to relieve their injustice (10.52–4). God commands the doing of justice and doing good to others (16.90). God loves those who do justice (60.80), and judges are commanded by God always to act justly between litigants. Above all (3.18) God bears witness that there is no God but God, and (so do) the angels and those possessed of knowledge who all proclaim that God maintains God's creation with justice.

Worship of God is directly related to the idea of acting justly in all dealings, whether with family, friends or strangers. There is probably no other notion so closely associated with God or with the will of God than justice. Lack of justice is anathema to God and goes against the central principles of all religions, though different religions define justice differently.

Christians, Jews and Muslims all look to Abraham as a pivotally important figure. Abraham was the father of the Jewish nation, and all Jews see themselves as descended from him. For Christians, Abraham is the father of faith – the person who staked his whole life on faith in the one, unseen God. In Islam,

Abraham is the first Muslim, the first monotheist and the first person to submit to Allah. Abraham's importance and his influence cannot be overestimated. Yet it is Abraham, above all other figures, who is shown in the Hebrew Scriptures as arguing with God and challenging God's right to impose an arbitrary judgement. It is Abraham who appeals to God against God's own command by reference to a higher and independent standard – and that standard is justice.

The story is a famous one but it is worth retelling because it goes to the heart of the distinction between 'good' and 'bad' religion:

> And the LORD said (to Abraham), Because the cry of Sodom and Gomorrah is great, and because their sin is very grievous; I will go down now, and see whether they have done altogether according to the cry of it, which is come unto me; and if not, I will know. And the men turned their faces from thence, and went toward Sodom: but Abraham stood yet before the LORD. And Abraham drew near, and said, Wilt thou also destroy the righteous with the wicked? Peradventure there be fifty righteous within the city: wilt thou also destroy and not spare the place for the fifty righteous that are therein? That be far from thee to do after this manner, to slay the righteous with the wicked: and that the righteous should be as the wicked, that be far from thee: Shall not the Judge of all the earth do right? And the LORD said, If I find in Sodom fifty righteous within the city, then I will spare all the place for their sakes. And Abraham answered and said, Behold now, I have taken upon me to speak unto the Lord, which am but dust and ashes: Peradventure there shall lack five of the fifty righteous: wilt thou destroy all the city for lack of five? And he said, If I find there forty and five, I will not destroy it. And he spake unto him yet again, and said, Peradventure there shall be forty found there. And he said, I will not do it for forty's sake. And he said unto him, Oh let not the Lord be angry, and I will speak: Peradventure there shall thirty be found there. And he said, I will not do it, if I find thirty there. And he said, Behold now, I have taken upon me to speak unto the Lord: Peradventure there

shall be twenty found there. And he said, I will not destroy it for twenty's sake. And he said, Oh let not the Lord be angry, and I will speak yet but this once: Peradventure ten shall be found there. And he said, I will not destroy it for ten's sake. (Genesis 18.20–32, AV)

In this story, Abraham argues with God. This, in itself, is extraordinary. When Abraham is later told to sacrifice his son with his wife, Sarah, he does not argue. The son he was called to sacrifice was the son of promise – the son for whom Abraham and his wife Sarah had waited all their lives. This was the son born long after Sarah was past child-bearing age, the son God had promised Abraham would be the father of innumerable descents. This was the son through whom Abraham's name would live on through succeeding generations, yet this was the same son God commanded Abraham to kill. Argument on Abraham's part would have been entirely reasonable and appropriate but he remained silent, did not speak to his wife Sarah, and set off with his son on a three-day journey that was planned to culminate in the son's death. Not once did Abraham question or argue – yet when God says that God intends to destroy the people of Sodom, Abraham argues. The grounds for his argument are not his own self-interest, as would have been the case if he had pleaded for the life of his son. Abraham argues with God because God is refusing to act justly. God is the Lord of the universe and God must act justly. As Abraham says, 'Shall not the judge of all the earth do right?' When God says that God intends to destroy innocent people in Sodom along with the guilty, Abraham argues. Abraham pleads for justice as God cannot act against God's own nature – the judge of the world must act justly. Abraham persuades God not to destroy the town if there are first 50, then 45, then 40, then 30, then 20 and finally ten just people in the town. However imprudent it may be to argue with the sovereign Lord of the Universe, however foolish – Abraham argues. How can the God of the whole universe deal unjustly? This goes to the heart of the issues in this book. Any religion that rejects justice and affirms that God's will is against justice must be bad religion.

Of course, this raises the question of 'whose justice', and this is not easy to determine. Almost no one thinks that they act unjustly – almost everyone (and almost every religious group) is able to convince themselves that their actions are just. However, being convinced that one's actions are just is not the same as their being just. This raises the question of whether there is such a thing as an absolute standard of justice.

Absolute justice

Plato argued for the absolute idea of justice, and Anselm of Canterbury, in the *Monologion,* drew on Plato in the prologue to his famous Ontological Argument. Plato lists a series of acts and then asks his listeners and readers to rank these, putting the most just acts first and the least just last. The list Anselm gives is as follows:

1. the one who plots injustice and carries it out;
2. the one who does not plot but, when the opportunity arises, does injustice;
3. the one who does justice expecting a reward;
4. the one who does justice, whether he gets reward or not;
5. the one who does justice, though he is mocked, stripped and has his eyes burned out and is impaled.

Plato and Anselm are in no doubt that everyone will be able to carry out this ranking, and this, he maintains, points to the existence of a universal understanding of justice. In any primary or junior school playground, if one listens long enough, a little voice will often be heard shouting in an aggrieved voice, 'It's not fair.' Young children have an innate capacity to recognize injustice. Indeed, one of the things that will make any child most aggrieved against a teacher is if the teacher is not fair and, for instance, has favourites. Justice is a deeply embedded notion. It is of course possible to convince oneself that one is being just when one isn't, but on reflection, on discussion with others and when a sincere attempt is made to understand alternative positions, it will be clear to most people where justice lies.

Not everyone will of course accept that justice is an absolute. In a postmodern and relativistic age, many will see justice as an entirely relativistic notion, just as the idea of truth and goodness may be held to be relative to culture. There is no one thing that postmodernism is, but most broadly it is a denial of any metanarrative – any single way of looking at truth and reality. Postmodernism in the twentieth century has eroded all previous certainties and has undermined faith in religion. However, religion precisely rejects the postmodern claim. In an extraordinary Papal encyclical called *Veritatis Splendor*, Pope John Paul II analysed the chief problem facing the modern world, which he saw not, as one might have expected, as being globalization, climate change, materialism or consumerism, but rather as the relativistic tide sweeping the world that has eroded past certainties and devalued the currency of faith. As we have seen previously (see p. 82), another encyclical, *Fides et Ratio*, provided a ringing endorsement for the importance of philosophy and, indeed, for philosophy to have autonomy in seeking out answers to the deeper questions of life. It deplored the increasing lack of interest by philosophy in the fundamental questions of meaning at the heart of human existence, and argued the need for philosophy to recapture the vision of the ancient Greeks in seeking truth about meaning and purpose. Justice was one of the central themes of the Greeks and of most philosophy. Until the modern era everyone accepted that justice was an absolute value, and the idea that justice is a purely relativistic notion is a modern phenomenon. If anyone denies this, possibly the most effective way of persuading him or her is to act unjustly towards them and wait to see how long it takes them to complain of injustice.

Probably in no other area do religions stand so closely together on the other side of a great divide. On one side stand postmodernism and relativism, rejecting any absolute idea of truth, justice or what is good and, on the other, united, almost every religion in affirming the centrality of absolute standards of justice, truth and goodness. Religion proclaims the central importance of justice, and this can provide an important way of demarcating good from bad religion. Good religion will be willing to engage in a discussion about the nature of justice and how it should be administered, will be passionately interested in working to bring justice, even working with those of other faiths and none to bring justice to all people. There are commonalities in the concepts and administrations of justice held by major religions, and good religion will seek to uncover and build on these. Those religions that fail to take justice seriously are bad religions and those that honestly and dispassionately seek to foster justice are good.

Critics will, of course, argue that justice is acting as God wants one to act and, therefore, if a religious group is acting according to what it sees as the will of God, it is acting justly. However, this is to go back to the problem outlined in Chapter 3 on the Euthyphro dilemma: justice does not just depend on God's whim as an arbitrary power figure. Justice lies at the heart of the rationality of the universe, and as God is held to have created the universe, so Justice depends on God in so far as it is part of the structure of the universe – but this does not mean to say that God's mere whim determines what is just. It is precisely this point that is made by Abraham when he argues with God. God has made God's will clear, but Abraham argues because God's proclaimed will is clearly unjust.

Immanuel Kant is one of the greatest and most important modern philosophers, and the central premise on which his entire philosophy rests is that the universe is rational. Not everyone, of course, accepts the rationality of the universe, but almost all religions claim that the universe is intelligible and understandable. If this is so, morality and justice are part of the fabric of the universe. Justice is not random, it is not arbitrary – it is something to be sought, discovered, stood for and affirmed in spite of all the voices that would suppress it. Justice is one of the most important tests of the validity of good religion. Where justice is absent so is good religion, and where injustice triumphs so does atheism and bad religion.

Aristotle defined justice as 'reason free from passion', by which he meant emotion, partiality and self-interest. Justice requires people to be dispassionate – to see what is right rather than what is easy, expedient or convenient; to be willing to act against one's own best interests or the interests of the group to which one belongs because justice is seen as demanding this. This means practising detachment – seeing clearly and well what is just and right, impartially and objectively, detached from one's interest or perspective.

The medieval Christian mystical writer, Meister Eckhart, praised detachment more than anything else:

> An authority called Avicenna says: 'The excellence of the spirit which has achieved detachment is so great that whatever it contemplates is true, and whatever it desires is granted, and whatever it commands one must obey.' And you should know that this is really so; when the free spirit has attained true detachment, it compels God to its being . . . And the man who has attained this complete detachment is so carried into eternity that no transient thing can move him, so that he experiences nothing of whatever is bodily, and he calls the world dead, because nothing earthly has any savor for him. This is what Saint Paul meant when he said: 'I live, and yet I do not; Christ lives in me' (Ga. 2:20).[1]

Detachment forces one to be free from prejudice, to judge dispassionately. It is a central part of rendering justice; Aristotle said that true law is 'reason free from passion'. The judge in a court case must be detached and must be ruled out of involvement in the case if he or she has any personal interest in it. Justice demands detachment and means that one must always be exceptionally wary of judging the justice of one's own case because judgement is too easily clouded by self-interest.

---

1 'On Detachment', in *Meister Eckhart: The Essential Sermons, Commentaries, Treatises, and Defense*, translation and introduction by Edmund Colledge OSA and Bernard McGinn, Classics of Western Spirituality, New York: Paulist Press, 1981, p. 288.

Justice and conflict

Augustine of Hippo wrote at a time when the Roman Empire had just become Christian and, in particular, he set out the idea of a just war – when and how wars should be fought. His ideas have come down to us in the present day and underpin most notions of justice in war. Wars, Augustine declared, must be fought without hatred and in order to restore justice and peace. They must also be ordered by a legitimate authority which, in previous ages, was seen as the nation state but today is increasingly seen as the United Nations – it is held that only the UN can be detached in making judgements about justice. The way any war is fought must, Augustine maintained, show justice – in particular in differentiating between innocents and combatants. Innocent life may never be taken directly, regardless of the purpose in doing so. The first of these criteria, that war must be undertaken without hatred, may seem almost amusing if not ridiculous. Surely, it will be argued, warfare necessarily involves killing, and this involves hatred? Augustine would reject this. Sometimes it may be necessary to fight to restore peace and justice, but war must always be undertaken with regret, and the humanity of those who are killed must be respected. Once nations fail in this, they become like animals and justice is not served. Sadly, today this is often ignored and the importance of the justice of conflicts often marginalized.

Augustine argued that a legitimate authority was required for war to be just. One of the major weaknesses of his analysis of just war thinking was the presumption he made that any legitimate authority would act with justice. In his eyes, obedience to the authority of the Christian Roman Emperor and the preservation of what, in his time, had become the Christian Roman state were prerequisites for justice, although he also clearly set out the need for a separate criterion of justice apart from legitimate authority. Sadly, these two requirements – of justice and authority – became conflated, throughout European history. Too often obedience to the King or Queen, supposedly God's anointed, was taken as legitimate grounds for believing a conflict to be just and for engaging in it. This, however, was a mistake. Many monarchs acted with scant regard for justice, and the Church, by failing to separate the need for, on the one hand, legitimate authority and, on the other, the requirement of justice, led people to assume that if the leader or leaders of a nation declared war, this ensured justice. The Church supported a feudal structure of society in which those lower down the social ladder owed a duty of obedience to their feudal lord. People were not encouraged to question and to challenge but to obey.

In the First and Second World Wars some few brave individuals stood out against the idea of authority being supreme by holding to pacifist principles. They rejected the justice of the war that was being fought but, all too generally, the assumption has been that if a nation declares war, the people of that nation should fight and regard the war as just. This was even more the case when the Church blessed the justice of a war (as it has frequently done). In these cases, any dispassionate analysis of the issue of justice was often ignored.

In the Kosovo conflict, NATO intervened for the best of reasons and in the interests of justice. After the collapse of communism in the Balkans, nationalism was whipped up by politicians, and the Serbs embarked on a campaign of racial cleansing, genocide and rape against the Muslim population of Kosovo. The UN was unable to intervene as both Russia and China threatened vetoes (the five permanent members of the Security Council all have the power of veto over any UN decision). Russia had long been an ally of Serbia, which shares with it an Orthodox Christian heritage, while China did not want the principle established of intervention in the internal affairs of a country on human-rights grounds. As the killing and rapes continued, it was left to NATO forces to intervene and to force the withdrawal of the Serb forces. This is one reasonably clear modern example of an attempt to enforce justice by force of arms. Sadly, however, this rarely happens, and in many cases instead of justice being served, the interests of the powerful and strong dominate. When 800,000 Tutsis were massacred in Rwanda, the world did nothing because no Western interests were seen to be involved and the people being killed were black and considered to be of little consequence. When the United States and Britain invaded Iraq, the excuse was that Saddam Hussein had weapons of mass destruction. No such weapons were found, and many speculated that the real motive for the war had nothing to do with justice but was, rather, concerned with American self-interest and oil.

For millions in the Islamic world, while the West may talk about the values of justice and freedom it is seen as mere rhetoric designed to disguise blatant self-interest. President George W. Bush used, unfortunately, the language of a crusade to describe the invasion of Iraq, and the invasion was seen by many in the United States as a just and righteous war. For many others it was the reverse of this – justice was not seen to be being done. The war was fought to prevent what Saddam Hussein's government might do in the future, despite little evidence of its intention to act in the manner claimed or of its capacity to do so. As countless tens of thousands of Iraqis died, there was – in all too many cases – little respect shown for them by the invading forces. The idea of this being in any sense a just war was seriously undermined. Iraqis were tortured and degraded, and some in the invading forces seemed to have little respect or care for the lives of Iraqi civilians. In so far as religion was, by some, seen to endorse this sort of conflict, it was an example of bad religion. If justice is not served, evil triumphs, and this applies even if the so-called justice is imposed in the name of religion.

If the West actually did stand for justice instead of self-interest, it would have a moral authority that, to many, it today lacks. The same applies to Christianity. If it is seen as standing for what is just or right, rather than supporting so-called Christian governments in what is seen by many as blatant self-interest, it might recover the moral authority it has long claimed but generally lost. Moral authority is directly linked to practising justice, even when it goes against one's own interests. Justice is not comfortable, it is not easy, but where it is not present, evil triumphs. The moral authority of religion is essential – and this authority is to be found not so much in disputed attitudes to issues such as sexual morality or stem-cell research, but in standing for justice even when this means acting against one's own interests. Good religion prospers by standing on the side of justice, even when it is inconvenient and inexpedient.

In the Middle Ages, several crusades were waged against 'the Infidel' – Muslim armies that occupied sites in Jerusalem revered by Christians. Itinerant preachers travelled across Europe whipping up a ferment of hatred against Muslims, who were regarded as almost subhuman. Indeed, while Christianity generally felt that there was a duty to convert non-Christians to Christian belief, this did not generally apply to Muslims, who were regarded as not worthy of conversion. This hatred of Muslims was widely shared across Europe, and support for it was given by large elements of the established Church. Few dared or cared to consider the justice of the situation, or whether Muslims might have as much right as Christians to be present in what is now Palestine. There was a general consensus that fighting in the crusades was God's will and that anyone who died on crusade was guaranteed a place in paradise. Hardly any voices were raised in dissent from this view – but one man set an example by challenging this whole intellectual paradigm of hatred. This was Francis of Assisi.

Chapter 16 of Francis' Earlier Rule (1221) for the Franciscan Order, which he founded, is concerned with the nature of the Franciscan brothers' missionary work, particularly in Islamic lands. It begins with the scriptural quotation, 'I am sending you out as lambs in the midst of wolves' (Luke 10.3). Much of the crusading propaganda spoke of Muslims as 'wolves' and 'beasts'. Francis and the brothers themselves had shared this cultural image. But they were to discover through their engagement with Islam that such images were wrong. Francis himself travelled, with one companion, to Egypt, where the Muslim and Christian forces confronted each other. Francis tried to persuade the crusaders to make peace but he was mocked and derided. He therefore secretly crossed the battle lines and was captured by the Muslim soldiers, who took him to their leader, the Sultan. Francis spent three days in discussion with the Sultan about God, prayer and the purpose of life. It was clear that both men made a profound impression on each other. The

Sultan had Francis returned safely to the Christian lines, and the meeting had a great effect on Francis. He later said that his followers were to regard Muslims not simply as friends but as brothers. This was a profound reversal of all the normal categories, but Francis went further. When he heard that another crusade was to be undertaken he went aside to conduct a long, fasting retreat, praying for protection for the Sultan, his friend. The crusades were absolutely the reverse of everything Francis stood for. Francis saw God in everyone and in every part of the natural world and he embraced all humanity – starting at the beginning of his ministry, when he embraced a leper. Francis and the Sultan in many ways stand for all that is best about religion – they are an excellent example of good religion at its best. The crusaders who ignored him, as well as those in power who launched and promoted the crusades, were in the wrong and were examples of bad religion, however sincere their aims may have been. Sincerity cannot make right what is wrong, nor can it make good what is bad. Sincerity is all too often present in bad religion but this cannot excuse its badness.

Today some Muslims feel a similar hatred of Western powers which, they believe, side with Israel in perpetuating what they see as an unjust occupation of the West Bank, parts of East Jerusalem and the Golan Heights – none of which were part of the territory originally ceded to Israel by the UN at the time of its formation. They were conquered by Israel following an attack on the state by Egypt, Syria and Jordan – the Israeli forces were incredibly efficient and effective and not only destroyed the forces of their attackers but also occupied significant parts of their territory against specific UN resolutions.

Many ordinary Muslims see Christians as identified with Western self-interest and are prepared to engage in what a minority see as Jihad or Holy War against Christian interests – sometimes burning churches and killing Christians (as in Iraq, Indonesia and Nigeria), sometimes carrying out terrorist attacks, as in 9/11 in New York or 7/7 in London, as well as elsewhere. Those who carry out such attacks see themselves as using the few weapons at their disposal and being assured of paradise if they die in the attempt because they regard themselves as carrying out God's will. Indeed, suicide bombers are willing to sacrifice their own lives freely and with joy because they feel they are assured of a heavenly reward. Both these attacks and the crusades are good examples of bad religion in action – although it must be said that the hatred of the crusaders for the Muslims was far more widely shared than is the hatred of a very small minority of Muslims today against the West and Christianity. Hardly any Christians spoke out at the time against the injustice of the crusades, and too few Muslims today are willing to speak out clearly against the injustice of terrorist attacks or, for instance, the rape, murder and genocide of Christians and animists in Darfur. The same applies in tensions and conflicts between Hindus and Muslims in India and Pakistan and the border country of Kashmir, where religious differences have been the cause of constant killings since independence from Britain in 1947 and where two nuclear-armed states face each other in a military stand-off that may yet have devastating consequences. Religion has too often accentuated hatred and suspicion, while justice has not been a priority for either side.

Confronting injustice

Silence in the face of injustice makes bad religion complicit in evil. Too many supposedly good Christians in Nazi Germany were silent before, and therefore complicit in, the Holocaust or Shoah. At the time, the leaders of the Lutheran and Catholic Churches were largely silent about the atrocities that were taking place and thereby were complicit in acts of unspeakable evil, as were the people who participated in these acts or the countless thousands of others who knew about them but remained silent. In the case of paedophilia in the Catholic Church, the official response has all too often been silence and a wish to protect the institution rather than engage with the evils taking place. Once institutional religion is given priority over justice, bad religion is almost certain to result.

The conviction that one is doing God's will when injustice is perpetrated is an example of bad religion. It is using religion for unjust ends, and those who contribute are complicit in the evil. It is not acceptable to move from saying, 'I feel sure this is God's will' to saying, 'This is God's will.' If God's supposed will is seen as calling people to act against justice, it must be rejected. Injustice cannot come from God. Plato was right in the Euthyphro dilemma that the authority of an autocrat, even a divine autocrat, cannot render just what is unjust. Abraham was right to challenge God when it looked as though God would act unjustly. God is praised and worshipped precisely because God is seen to stand for justice. Once religion denies this it has become corrupt – a tool for the powerful to exploit the gullible for selfish ends. Marx's analysis that religion is the opium of the masses is, sadly, too often correct – when religion is used as a tool by those with power to maintain and enhance their position against those who are weak and powerless. However, instead of rejecting all religion, Marx – like other atheists – should have instead sought to differentiate between good and bad religion.

Justice requires dispassionate, rational analysis. It requires seeing both sides of a case. It is directly related to fairness. Justice may not always be easily discernible, but where people of good will can put aside self-interest it should be achievable and recognizable. Of course, justice is an ideal and ideals cannot always be actualized – but the ideal nevertheless remains. Merely because the ideal cannot be reached in its fullness does not invalidate it. Religion should always strive towards this idea of justice, and when it fails to do so it should be condemned as unfaithful to its own central principles. The willingness to seek and to do justice is, therefore, a crucial litmus test in any attempt to separate good and bad religion.

9

Equality

Religion and humanity

By their nature, religions claim that those who believe in them are 'better' than those who do not. One of the most difficult issues in religion is therefore how to treat non-believers and members of other faiths. Both believers and non-believers are human beings, so treatment of non-believers is a test of a religion's basic attitude to human life. Most religions value human life, and believe in its essential sanctity. God created and has an interest in human life regardless of its form or what an individual has or has not done. Killing or even hurting a human being deliberately and without just reason is a grave sin in most religions, regardless of the beliefs of the victim. Most religions are also open, willing to share the truth they claim to possess with any person who is interested, so giving them a chance to believe and achieve any reward or salvation on offer.

It is clear that while most religions have a basic respect for human life, not all do. Some religious leaders have preached that killing non-believers could be acceptable or even a religious duty. The book of Samuel records the prophet Samuel telling King Saul that he should kill non-Israelite prisoners of war, including women and children, and then telling Saul that he had lost God's favour when he did not go this far. In 1098 Pope Urban II preached the first crusade and told Christians that they could atone for all their sins and thus have a chance of going straight to heaven if they joined the Church's army and killed Muslims. The Qur'an seems to teach that those who do not believe in God or are polytheistic deserve a fate worse than death, although the context of this passage may have a bearing on its meaning. Most people would accept that waging war purely to expand the influence of a religion, to exterminate 'the competition' or those whose beliefs are incompatible with one's own but who do not pose any other threat, would be wrong. The basic principles of 'just war' described in the previous chapter would rule out launching attacks without good reason, let alone using unjust means, such as killing prisoners of war, women and children or using torture. These principles, though most famously set out by Augustine, are set out in Islamic texts as well and are in accordance with many passages from the Hebrew Scriptures and New Testament.

Killing non-believers is arguably justified when a religion is under attack, but what might constitute 'attack' is debatable. For Mossad, the Israeli secret service, killing the enemies of Israel (howsoever defined) is justified by the country's being in a perpetual state of war with its neighbours, and the existence of anti-Semites all over the world. For members of Al-Qaeda, 'anti-Islamic' Western political and economic policy constitutes sufficient grounds to make killing non-Muslim civilians just. Most people regard these arguments as invalid and the killing of non-believers as unjust, basically as actions stemming from self-interest (see the previous chapter on justice).

Identifying religion with race or nationality causes particular problems. Most obviously it means that religion is more likely to be dragged into secular conflicts, and once involved it can be misused and can heighten tensions, making resolutions almost impossible to reach.

In Ireland the roots of the 'Troubles' were in the policies applied by the British in trying to annex Ireland, not as an equal part of Great Britain but effectively as a colony to be used for its resources. British attempts to conquer and colonize its neighbour have a long and bloody history, but really got going when Britain became a Protestant country, while Ireland remained Catholic. King William IV followed his military campaign against the Irish with a policy of forced resettlement, moving Protestant Scots into the North of Ireland, installing English Aristocrats and Anglican

clergymen as mostly absentee 'landowners' (making the peas-
antry into serfs) and taking Irish Catholics out of towns and
cities to use as forced labour overseas. Irish resentment against
the British was easily translated into Catholic resentment against
Protestants. British contempt for the Irish was easily translated
into Protestant contempt for Catholics. National characteristics
were mixed up with religious doctrines in a confused mass of
propaganda, passed down the generations and still in evidence
today. To those brought up with this inheritance it seems reasonable to throw stones at Catholic children as they walk to their
primary schools or to shoot a policeman because of a Protestant
symbol on his badge. Elsewhere in the world Roman Catholics
and Anglicans or Presbyterians engage in dialogue, even using
the same liturgy – Common Worship – since 2000, but in Northern Ireland members of each community often demonize the
other, and there is little the Churches can do to prevent their
names being used as an excuse.

  In Israel the identification of religion with race and nationality has also caused problems. It has caused all Jews, men,
women and children alike, to be seen as fair targets by the op-
ponents of the state of Israel, despite the fact that Israel is a
democracy, that the majority of Israelis voted against the government and that more disagree with its more extreme policies.
The unfair lumping together of all Semitic people has been used
to excuse the unfair lumping together of all Arabic people; as
Deuteronomy commands: 'an eye for an eye and a tooth for
a tooth' (Deut. 19.21). Now it is routine for Arabs to have to
carry identity papers, to have their education, employment and
movements restricted *because they are Arab*, not because they
are Muslim or because they are Palestinian. Assumptions are
made about one's beliefs on the basis of one's appearance, and
appearance is used to justify dividing some people off for different, worse, treatment. It has been argued by some that this
is becoming close to the 'racial hygiene' policies enforced by
Nazis in Germany, policies that led to the Holocaust. Religion,
race, nationality and politics become dangerous when they
become entangled.

Judaism poses a very particular challenge in largely defining religion in terms of racial descent. This means that Judaism is naturally exclusive, generally does not proselytize and is therefore different in character from either Christianity or Islam. There are similarities with Sikhism, which is largely limited to those of Punjabi descent in practice, though there is no doctrinal necessity for this racial limitation in the way there is in Judaism. Liberal Jews have moved away from defining religion in this controversial way and now, in some communities, seek new members and routinely accept converts without the high hurdles and second-class status usually placed in front of proselytes in Orthodox and Reform synagogues. This has, however, meant that Liberal Jews are often not recognized as Jews at all by those from Orthodox or Reform traditions. Arguably, the identification of Jewishness with racial descent rather than creed places mainstream Judaism in a difficult position vis-à-vis a discussion about good and bad religion. If one is Jewish by birth there is little room for personal choice in religion; neither is there the openness that would offer any human being access to the truth and salvation the religion claims. The religion may seem elitist and may seem to give grounds for members to believe they are better than non-Jews. It may be used as an excuse for behaviour towards non-Jews that is unjust or that even ignores the value of their essential humanity. Clearly these eventualities have rarely been actualized on any large scale, but the potential for the misuse of Jewish doctrine must be highlighted and kept in mind by Jewish authorities and people. Perhaps it is partially in fear of what Jewish doctrine might legitimize that the seeds of anti-Semitism lie. Dialogue between Orthodox, Reform and Liberal Judaism would seem essential in keeping discussion and consideration of these points going, and Jewish representation in interfaith dialogue should include all these traditions, helping non-Jews to understand that a range of interpretations exists within the community.

Good religion must respect the essential value of human life, regardless of the beliefs of individuals. It can never support holy war or killing non-believers without unequivocal provocation.

Good religion should resist being dragged into political disputes, but this is not to say that religion should never be political. Good religions stand up for the search for truth, justice and equality, and must therefore engage in public debates when these issues are at stake. Nevertheless, they should not be used as cover by factions in national disputes; rather they should speak in their own voice on matters of principle. Good religion is usually open to anybody who is interested, offering fair access to the truth and salvation. Though there may be exceptions to this, these should be the subject of proper and continual discussions.

The particular issue of equality in Eastern religions

Eastern religions pose a particular problem when it comes to discussing the issue of equality. The world view within which they developed and now operate is markedly different from that common to Western Abrahamic religion. Most Hindus, Buddhists and Sikhs believe in reincarnation (*samsara*) and the law of *karma*, that is, that actions have consequences. Not only is the effect of actions felt within this life, but on a longer scale actions in one life will affect how one's soul (*atman*) is reborn. Therefore moral reward or punishment is in this world, though in a future body, not in 'heaven' or 'hell'. Hindus, Buddhists and Sikhs also accept the concept of *dharma* – that one's situation in, or time of, life implies certain expectations. Fulfilling these expectations accrues positive *karma* and failing to fulfil them accrues negative *karma*, either of which will have the appropriate future effect in this life or the next. It follows that if one is born into a lower *caste* and *varna* (class and profession), fulfilling the expectations associated with one's social position is good and breaking out by, for instance, trying to 'better oneself' could actually have the reverse effect when the negative *karma* generated takes its toll.

This world view has similarities with the concept of the 'body politick' so much beloved of Tudor writers in England. There are those who are born to be leaders and those born to be workers. Society prospers when people know their place, stick to it with good grace and work to the best of their abilities at their proper tasks. Of course, the Tudor concept of the body politick is drawn out of Platonic writings. Many passages, including the famous analogy of the charioteer in the *Phaedrus*, suggest that society has its brains, its passionate idealists and its strong arms, and should take from each according to their role and ability. In the writings of Plato, just as in some of the texts of Eastern religions, there is the idea that breaking out of one's natural role might destabilize society and even have negative consequences for oneself.

How then should the concept of equality be handled in the context of Eastern religions? If somebody is poor, disabled, a member of a disadvantaged ethnic group, a woman or homosexual, this may be seen as the result of *karma* from a previous life. People 'deserve' their lot and there may not be any imperative to ensure that criminals and prisoners have a pleasant life as their punishment is deserved. When faced with the issue of Dalits ('untouchables') in India, Gandhi observed that there is a difference between not seeking to alter somebody's basic situation and using that situation as an excuse for treating them unreasonably. In this there may be a way forward. When approaching the issue of equality within the context of Eastern religions it may be reasonable to suggest that all people should have the opportunity to accrue positive *karma* through fulfilling their *dharma* and in moral actions, so as to work towards more positive future incarnations. People should therefore have the right to fulfil their social role with dignity and a degree of personal liberty. Slavery in all its forms and the practice of ostracizing people should not be tolerated; people should have the responsibility to ensure that they treat other people with basic respect, acknowledging their existence, permitting them some free time, the ability to have and see their families, to learn and worship and to be paid reasonably for their work. Looking at the situation from the other side, treating people of all types well and respecting life is morally praiseworthy according to all Hindu, Buddhist and Sikh texts, and there must therefore be a karmic reward for taking one's responsibilities towards the less fortunate seriously.

It seems that insights drawn from Aristotelian philosophy may be useful when attempting to distinguish good religion from bad religion within the context of Eastern traditions. Aristotle does not suggest that it is more or less easy to flourish as a rich person than as a poor person, as a member of one race than another nor as a man than as a woman. As human beings we are fulfilled through living peacefully, prospering in our situation, acquiring wisdom and passing it on to the next generation. It is conceivable that one could do this as a baker as much as as a teacher, as a mother as much as as a father. Clearly it would be inappropriate for any person, policy or religious doctrine to stand in the way of people being able to flourish in this basic way – but that does not mean that all customs and traditions have to be abandoned, that a baker not seeking to become a teacher or a woman not seeking a professional career is wrong.

Religion and minorities

Religions' attitudes to those who by numbers and/or power are in a minority are directly related to their attitudes to justice in general, but are more complex and controversial. Across the world, governments and some religious authorities have signed up to UN initiatives that emphasize the equality of all human beings, irrespective of race, gender, sexual orientation, physical abilities or other differentiating factors. These ideals are not always supported at grass roots, but in theory at least, every country and most religions have recognized their importance.

Arguably these initiatives have been among the most important human developments of the last century and, in many cases, the catalysts for change have been inspired by their faith. International awareness of the injustice of colonialism and abuses of the caste system owed much to the actions and words of Gandhi, a Hindu, who drew inspiration from the words of the *Bhagavad Gita* and from insights gained through long periods of meditation, fasting and simple communal living. International awareness of the injustice of institutional racism owed a great deal to the actions and particularly the oratory of Martin Luther King Jr, a Baptist Pastor from Atlanta, Georgia. International awareness of the injustices fostered by Chinese policy in Tibet owes much to the actions and words of the Dalai Lama, a displaced and thus essentially powerless leader of Tibetan Buddhism. Despite the important role religion has had in inspiring change, religious authorities have not generally taken a lead in promoting or instigating measures to bring about equality.

Mainstream Christianity and Islam have both tolerated and, indeed, promoted slavery in the past. The Christian and Islamic scriptures contain no condemnation of it. Apartheid South Africa was a highly religious country where most people accepted and endorsed apartheid. The segregation of blacks and whites in the southern United States occurred in a society that was highly religious. The massacres in Rwanda happened in a culture in which religion dominated and did little to challenge or undermine the hatred and mutual suspicion between tribal groups. Hindu authorities have perpetuated a caste system whereby the accident of birth has maintained social control by the dominant group of those less fortunate (particularly Dalits). It is also true, however, that opposition to slavery and apartheid came primarily from those inspired by religion and that wherever there is conflict, violence and hatred there are occasional examples of religious people who bravely stand against their own culture in the interests of what is just and right.

We have here, therefore, yet another instance of the polarity between good and bad religion. Bad religion tends to tolerate and foster the status quo, whereas good religion challenges accepted practice in the name of justice and to call society to move forward beyond existing conventions. Thus religious commands can call people to act outside and against cultural norms, but should not run against a general consensus internationally of what counts as admirable moral behaviour, grounded in a common understanding of what it means to live a fulfilled human life.

However, this raises a problem. If it was good to challenge slavery when it was accepted by many religious people; if it was good to challenge apartheid and racial discrimination when it was accepted by many religious people; if it was good to challenge discrimination against disabled people when this was tolerated by many religious people – then what about the position of women and homosexuals (to give but two prominent examples)? Surely, it can be argued, all human beings are equal and, therefore, any discrimination on the grounds of gender and sexual orientation must be condemned and resisted by good religion, even if it is perpetuated and affirmed by bad religion. This is difficult territory!

Women

Women have traditionally not been treated equally by all religions. They have not been given a full role in worship. They have not in many cases been allowed to be priests or church leaders. Their contributions to philosophy, theology and learning have often been ignored, and their insights into mysticism and religious experience have been largely suppressed and overruled. Women have today taken their place as the equal of men in nearly every aspect of life, at least in the Western world. Women lead major corporations and governments and have become leading barristers, judges and parliamentarians – yet within many religions the position of women has changed little. Some women reject religion as a result, although it is also true that religion in the West tends to retain greater appeal among women than men. What are the intellectual grounds for religions continuing to discriminate against women? The answer is simple and twofold – first, tradition, and second, appeal to sacred texts. It is here that the argument of this book begins to bite and will be rejected by many. Appeal to tradition and to sacred texts to justify the supposed commands of God cannot, it has been argued, be permissible as the sole grounds for religious imperatives. There are too many problems raised by hermeneutics and interpretation for it to be possible to claim certainty about what God wants; to justify, for instance, women's subservient place by saying:

- In Christianity, Paul said that women should be silent in church.
- Paul said that the head of a woman should be a man, just as Christ is the head of the Church.
- Jesus chose only male apostles, so women should never be allowed to be priests.
- Periods have been associated with uncleanness, so a woman who might be menstruating should never be given Church leadership.
- Women cannot adequately represent human beings before God, and men are more perfectly formed in the image of God than women.
- In Islam, the Qur'an says that the witness of a woman in a court case does not equal that of a man.
- A woman, according to some versions of Islam, may not drive a car or go out of her house unaccompanied by a man or be alone with a man who is not her husband or a close relative.
- Women have to keep their bodies completely covered – sometimes with a mask so that even their eyes may not be seen – as they are a temptation to men.
- Men may divorce women but not the other way round.
- Women may not participate equally with men in Islamic or Jewish worship.
- Most Buddhist monasteries refuse to allow the entry of women.

These positions can no longer be straightforwardly accepted as so much depends on the culture in which such claims are made as well as a tradition stretching back for centuries. The supposed authority of God or sacred texts that are invoked in support can be questioned and challenged, and certainty about their application today cannot be achieved. 'God wants this' can easily become a substitute for 'this is the way it has always been'. All of the above claims can be and have been questioned but they are nevertheless still widely held. Challenges to them have been suppressed by the power and authority of religious bodies (themselves male-dominated) and discussion of them has often been banned.

However, it is one thing to claim that women are equal to men, it is another to hold that they are identical to men. Women can have babies and feed them, men cannot. Women have always invested more in the care and cherishing of families than have men. Some hold that women cannot have it all – hard choices have to be made between the role of wife and mother and the role of career woman. There are cultural differences here that are complex, and it is very easy to slip into a cultural imperialism that assumes that 'our culture is right' and that 'others are wrong'. Many would hold that the Western emphasis on women 'having it all' (in terms of the roles of wife, mother, career woman and independent social being) is unrealistic. There is some evidence to suggest that the 'sexual revolution' in the West has caused women today to be typically less fulfilled than their grandmothers were. Although some women have relished the opportunity to enter universities and the professions, have flourished and have contributed a great deal to society, this is not always the case. The shift from the expectation that women stay at home to the expectation that women work has meant that there are many more workers available. Simple laws of supply and demand mean that they are paid proportionately less as workers than when only men were available and those men had to support a family on their wages. Most families cannot manage without women working, and this means that having children is difficult. The birth rate is falling, the use of contraception is routine and the number of abortions is still rising. Women have to hand over tiny babies to their mothers or to nurseries, have to stop breastfeeding much earlier than health advice would support, have to impose 'controlled crying' techniques so that they can get uninterrupted sleep so as to be fresh in the office. Children become 'latch-key kids' from an early age, left to entertain themselves with televisions and computers (or to roam the streets without supervision) while both their parents work into the evenings. In many cases it seems that women's interests as mothers and, even more, the interests of their children, are not well served by the 'have it all' culture, and it is unlikely to contribute to human flourishing.

In terms of the discussion in this book, the claim that 'our culture is right' can too easily translate into 'our religious traditions are good' and 'others are mistaken or bad'. There is no universal agreement on issues here. Many women around the world cherish and value their role as wives and mothers more than any other achievements, and if some religions tend to support this model more than others, it does not make these religions bad. Even if there is a single set of qualities that lead to human flourishing, it does not follow that there is only one form of life (cultural milieu) that would enable those qualities or human flourishing to be fulfilled. Rich, poor, craftsman, priest, black, white, old, young, athlete, deaf, mother or father can all be 'good' people. The saints and moral heroes in world history have not all come from a single religious or cultural tradition. There may be different ways for societies to operate that offer equal opportunities for the individuals within them to flourish. Arguably, it may be as possible for women to be fulfilled within a society in which the norm is for women to make homes, as within a society that necessitates their having careers. However, even if some such differences in perceptions of the role of women are understandable and valid, others are not and need to be resisted and challenged.

What is essential is that women should not be prevented from fulfilling their full potential as human beings. Their rights to life and liberty should be taken as seriously as those of men. From such broad principles it is possible to derive some absolute requirements that need to be demanded from any religion that can be categorized as in any sense good.

First, woman should have equal access to basic education, which is itself a prerequisite for the human rights of either men or women to be meaningful. Without basic literacy and numeracy and the opportunity to learn the skills of survival, women cannot be in a position to keep themselves and their families safe, to participate in politics, to find work to support themselves should they need to do so, or to find out about their own gifts and talents and to make informed decisions about the sort of life they want to lead. The practice, for instance, in parts of Afghanistan of denying any education to women in the name of religion is an example of bad religion in action and should be challenged and resisted by all. The same practice used to be followed in Christianity when women were denied access to schools simply because they were women. Fatuous arguments were used to explain why women, who were intellectually quali-fied and prepared to pay the fees, could not enter universities or take degrees alongside men, and why they could not therefore access the professions. According to Victorian academics, many of them ordained, women were 'weak minded', subject to hys-teria when forced to think for too long and likely to suffer early physical collapse and infertility as a result. Such arguments have long been shown to be ridiculous. Denying women open access to basic education or the opportunity to enter further education or a career, where such opportunities exist for anybody, and if the women in question are able and so inclined, can no longer be acceptable.

Second, women should be able to determine the courses of their own lives, to make choices about marriage, children, ca-reer and so on, bounded only by the options that are available to any person in their society and not limited because they are women. Women should be encouraged to be free, autonomous human beings, which means that marriage should be something freely chosen and not coerced by family pressure. And within the marriage the rights of the woman should be equal to those of the man. What is more, women should not be married off when they are still effectively children. They must be able to make a decision for themselves, and this means that the age of consent for marriage cannot be the same as the age of puberty (which may only be ten years old). Rape, beatings and cruelty to women should be condemned and rejected. A man should not have the right to forcibly correct his wife nor to force himself sexually on her. Women should not be forced into a particular role, for in-stance by being coerced into simply doing housework (often used as a way of making pursuing education and a career impossible for them). Leadership roles in the workplace should not be ruled out simply because of gender.

Leadership roles in religion are more complex. Open debate should be able to take place about the role of women in religious life. Views should be able to be expressed without being stifled or subject to sanction. If religious authorities are really about communicating the truth, they should welcome questioning and have little problem in defending their position. Religious doctrines can and have developed and, in principle at least, it needs to be acknowledged that such development may take place in respect of the role of women. There is diversity within almost all religious groups about the position of women, and any religion that seeks truth and is willing to admit the possible errors of the past has to be open to its existing values and assumptions being questioned and challenged.

This leaves open complex issues of religious practice in which there is clear cultural diversity and in respect of which there is no single and agreed set of assumptions. Some religions allow multiple wives, others demand monogamy. Some religions permit divorce and remarriage, and others do not. These are issues on which there are legitimate differences – alternative positions may be held with both passion and integrity. It is perhaps significant that most world religions have seen women in leadership roles in the past – some of the most important figures in Jewish history have been women, and one woman, Deborah, was even a Judge of Israel (the nearest equivalent to a wartime leader). Jesus mixed with women freely, and women were among his closest friends and followers. Islam rejected female infanticide at a time when this was common, and allowed women to own property and to run their own businesses. However, this has not generally translated into religious leadership.

Some religions permit women in leadership roles, and others do not. Discussion on such issues is important and needs to continue in an open and informed way. Where religions refuse even to allow the possibility of discussion, this needs to be challenged and resisted. Discussion is not, of course, the same as acquiescence, and religious groups may have legitimate perspectives that deserve to be listened to and considered; but debate must be allowed and women's voices heard – even if they are not necessarily accepted. This can be challenging for any religion – when what is just and right goes against deeply imbedded religious and cultural values, passions are likely to be roused and anger and resentment encouraged. Every religious group is likely to retreat behind its own certainties and to proclaim the rightness of its present position and the wrongness of alternatives. To be willing, in humility, to accept that present long-accepted practices may need re-examination and revision will never be easy. It is always easier simply to reinforce the status quo and revert back to authoritarian interpretations of scripture and tradition.

Change is never easy, and in the religious arena that is more clearly the case than anywhere else – but good religion should precisely be open to the need to examine the possible need for change and development. There is no religion that has never changed its outlook or has never made mistakes in the past, and once it is acknowledged that mistakes have been made it is not defensible to ignore the possibility, in principle at least, that present outlooks may also be mistaken. There is a legitimate plurality of positions within different major world religions. Christians, Jews, Hindus, Muslims and others do not always agree on their attitudes to women, and unless the possibility exists of listening to others it is all too easy for each subgroup to retreat into its own certainties and condemn every other position as deviant and mistaken. Such a position implies an arrogance that sits badly with any claim to be an example of good religion in action.

Homosexuality

Homosexuality is another issue on which religious groups differ significantly, although there is broad condemnation of homosexual practice in most traditional religions. There are some dissenting voices, and some, mostly small, subgroups that accept such practice even in the lives of religious leaders. However, even in the case of these small subgroups, they would all accept that such practice can only be allowed within a long-term, committed homosexual or lesbian relationship and would rule out casual relationships. However, on the whole the vast majority of major religious groups are united in condemning homosexual practice. Yet if discrimination is to be rejected on all grounds, including sexual difference, should it not also be right to question those religions that condemn homosexual practice? As in most issues of ethics, there is no clear and decisive argument against homosexual practice. Of course, there are strong arguments that can be put forward, including that such practices are unnatural, that they go against revelation in almost every religion, that they are met with widespread revulsion by many in the majority community and that the purpose for which genitalia are supposedly intended can be held to be being misused. Nevertheless, none of these arguments is conclusive and all can be countered. It is true, for instance, that homosexuality is condemned in the Hebrew Scriptures, but so is wearing garments with mixed fabrics, masturbation or cutting one's hair. Women in the Hebrew Scriptures are required to marry their dead husband's brother and to have children with him, and there are purity laws that almost no one would accept today. In short, as we have seen, any text needs to be interpreted and some religious leaders, such as Rowan Williams the Archbishop of Canterbury, see no problem with a long-term, committed homosexual or lesbian relationship.

There is no clear way of demonstrating that homosexual practice is necessarily right and good and, therefore, no clear way of condemning religions that reject such behaviour as part of their belief system. However (and this is an important caveat), accepting that religions may condemn behaviour which they consider unacceptable – and this would include not just homosexuality but abortion, stem-cell research, IVF, euthanasia, divorce, pre-marital sex and similar issues – and accepting that religions may proclaim and argue their views regarding right and wrong behaviour forcibly and clearly is one thing, but allowing that they should be able to impose their views on others is altogether another. We have already seen that all religions seek truth and that all religions claim to have truth – but also that it is necessary to acknowledge that error is possible and that whatever views are held to be true today may be modified or rejected tomorrow. However great the certainty claimed by any given religion, there is an overriding requirement for humility. To impose sanctions, therefore, on those with a different faith perspective, who do not share the same convictions as a given group, must be an example of bad religion in practice. A devout Catholic may, permissibly, condemn homosexual behaviour and refuse to practise such behaviour himself, but must be willing to acknowledge that other Christian denominations to not share this conviction. A devout Muslim may absolutely condemn alcohol and refuse drink, but must accept that many other religions see no problem with the moderate use of alcohol. Religion needs to work by persuasion, not coercion.

This raises the important question of how far religious conviction should be allowed to intrude into the public space. In a democracy, alternative perspectives can and should be argued, and this includes diverse religious perspectives. If laws are made by a majority, if the majority can be persuaded to agree to laws that rule out certain behaviour, it may be morally acceptable that they should be passed, provided they do not interfere with certain internationally agreed standards. The latter is an important caveat: there have been too many examples of laws passed that were accepted by a majority (such as in Nazi Germany, in the southern United States when slavery ruled and in Saudi Arabia today, where women's freedom is extremely curtailed) but that were nevertheless abhorrent and should have been and need to be rejected. In a civilized society the understanding of what behaviour may be morally tolerated can develop and change over time. Religious voices must be heard as part of this debate but, in the final analysis, religious opinions must not be allowed to dominate simply because they have a certain degree of authority. It follows that where religions move into the political sphere, and where states become effectively dominated by religion, concern to protect those who differ from the dominant religious view needs to be very great. If the power of the controlling religious authorities is used to subjugate alternative views, suppress dissenting voices and forcibly ensure compliance with its own edicts, these are pointers to bad religion. Christian Churches have long used their political power to impose agendas that would today be condemned. Muslim authorities in some countries suppress dissent and impose a uniformity steming from a narrow view of Islam. Such attempts need to be challenged and resisted. They have more to do with structures of power than with any search for truth, and are notably lacking in the humility that is part of any good religion.

Ethics is not black and white; there are many shades of grey. However, religions tend not to operate well where such shades exist. In practice, the tendency is for religions to teach that certain actions are absolutely right and others absolutely wrong. It is important to notice that the focus is on actions, not on the people carrying them out. It is much easier to communicate a list of prohibitions to a congregation than to explain the particular insight a religion offers into what it means to live a good life and why that would mean doing some things and not doing others. Perhaps doing what is easier and more practical, reducing religious ethics into a list of 'thou shalt nots', has led even religious authorities to forget that discussions about right and wrong, good and bad, should be much more complex. Jesus noted that the law was given to serve mankind, not mankind the law, and this might be a salutary comment in respect to Christianity today as well as many other religious traditions. How many disputes are over the letter of one regulation appearing to contradict the letter of another? How many could be resolved by looking to the spirit of the law and thinking about the interests of the people concerned, about the real lives affected? Good religion should always consider the agents as well as the actions in ethics, be willing to discuss and consider the reasons for prohibitions, and should not expect people to be satisfied with blanket bans, texts quoted without reference to context or the argument 'it has always been that way'.

Protecting the unborn

Kant described human beings as ends in themselves and infinitely precious. All religions affirm this but bad religion sometimes ignores what it really means, seeking to coerce others to their understanding of truth. It is the contention of this book that such coercion is wrong. If religion must be free from coercion (unless the rights of others are to be protected), what then about abortion? Many religious people will claim that killing a foetus is absolutely wrong: the foetus is a person and deserves protection. Here, it may be claimed, that is an absolute moral demand that must be enforced in the public space because of both a religious demand and the need to protect the innocent. This is of course a controversial area, and it depends on two key issues:

- Whether the foetus is, indeed, a person. Opinions differ on this. In Christianity it was traditionally held that a person was not formed until God implanted a soul which, according to Augustine, was 40 days after the conception of a male and 90 days in the case of a female. This position was changed by Pope John Paul II, and the Catholic Church now holds that human life begins at conception – but this is a change from the previous position. In Islam, the status of the foetus changes when God is said to implant a soul (either at 100 or 120 days after conception).
- Whether it can ever be right to do a wrong act. Sometimes, proportionalists will argue, there may be a proportionate reason that means that it is right to do a wrong act because there is a reason (or reasons) of sufficient gravity that outweighs the wrongness of the act. For instance, it may be right to lie in order to save the life of an innocent person. Similarly there may be proportionate reasons that make it the right thing to do to abort. For instance, if a pregnancy is the result of rape or the mother's life is in danger, these could be proportionate reasons to argue that the wrongness of abortion is outweighed by the gravity of the other reasons.

Alternative positions on these issues are held with conviction and compassion by some religious groups, although they may be in the minority. Nevertheless, they are legitimate views that can and should be argued. The issues are not straightforward, and this is where ethics again enters the world of greys rather than black and white.

Alternative views need to be listened to with compassion and openness, but there are not sufficiently agreed criteria to maintain that a religion is either good or bad simply by reference to their attitudes to particular ethical issues, for instance abortion. Rather, reference may be made to the way in which religions engage in ethical debate and whether this is done in a spirit of openness to alternative views, with humility and compassion and, perhaps above all, with respect and an attempt at understanding for people having to wrestle with hard ethical decisions. Where this is absent, religion may be seen to veer towards becoming bad religion. Certainty in moral questions is attractive but it is also dangerous, particularly when religious claims in ethics have, in the past, been shown to be flawed. Fundamentalism will react to the increase in relativism by becoming increasingly strident and assertive and by seeking to enforce by any means its own understanding of what is morally right or wrong. It is precisely this stridency and the lack of balance that needs to be resisted. This does not mean that there are no ethical absolutes but rather that in the search for what is good, right and just, alternatives need to be considered. To refer back to Chapter 2 on truth, just because one believes that there is a truth does not mean to say that one believes that this truth is or can be known, let alone with certainty. It may be that our various ethical principles are versions of, approximations at, a greater truth. No religion or society has a complete or objective understanding of what it is to be human, and no language can perfectly convey revealed truths. While we may move closer to an understanding of which actions contribute to human flourishing and which actions diminish human beings and take them further from fulfilment, it may not be possible to arrive at any single set of moral values.

10

Freedom

Freedom is an essential prerequisite for 'good religion' – as it is for morality. Unless human beings are free in a genuine, non-determined sense, the idea of choosing to serve and worship God or some higher order makes no sense.

Many today deny human freedom and would claim that, if we understood enough about the forces acting on human beings (both internal and external), we would understand that all human beings are actually completely determined. In the twentieth century, behavioural psychology argued for this and, more recently, evolutionary psychology maintains that all human dispositions and actions can be explained by inherited, evolved behaviour. Just as Darwinian natural selection can explain the evolution of human bodies, so the evolution of human emotional and moral responses can be explained in evolutionary terms. Taboos against incest have, it is claimed, evolved from the primates from whom all human beings are descended, in order to protect the human gene pool. Altruism and love are simply evolved behaviour patterns that have been developed over countless generations to foster the survival of the human gene pool – people are more altruistic to those most closely related to them genetically. Such an analysis denies human freedom and the capacity for human beings to be able to make morally autonomous and originating decisions. The word 'originating' is important here – it means that individual humans can be the originating, source of actions that are not determined by their past conditioning, whether this be genetic or cultural.

Religion crucially depends on freedom. Those who hold that human beings can be originating sources of action argue that we are individually accountable for our actions. Such freedom and responsibility is necessary when religions claim that people will be judged according to the way they have believed or behaved. Without freedom, humans cannot justly be held responsible for their beliefs or actions, as most religions claim they are. If a religion teaches that human beings are not free and yet are still responsible, that teaching seems false. If a religion acts to restrict individual freedoms, it may be restricting individual responsibility as well. It may claim that in restricting freedom it seeks to protect people from the consequences of sin, but the flip-side of this may be that they stand in the way of possible reward and/or salvation. Belief in human freedom is, therefore, a necessary corollary of good religion.

Sadly not all religious groups accept this. Some maintain that a particular race is a 'chosen people', selected by God and given preference before other groups. Here what matters is not a freely chosen act of obedience but rather lineal descent. Under this understanding, an accident of birth justifies one group of human beings rather than others – personal autonomy and decision making are of secondary importance. The principle of the fundamental equality of all human beings is radically undermined, and the accident of birth or culture determines whether or not one belongs to the group that is regarded as religiously acceptable. Judaism makes precisely this claim although, surprisingly, it was a claim specifically challenged in the story of Jonah.

Initially, the prophet Jonah firmly believed that God cared only for the people of Israel. He was forced through prolonged suffering to accept the fact that the people of Nineveh, whom he had regarded as outcasts and rejected by God, fit only for divine destruction, were cared for by God as much as the people of Israel. God was the God of Nineveh and not just Israel. It was a painful conclusion for him, but the whole story of Jonah is about his being forced to come to this realization. It is one thing, of course, to be a chosen people in terms of being a light to the world and an example to other nations, and to this extent Judaism may claim a unique and important place. The survival of the people of Israel, in spite of great persecution and every attempt to stamp them out, is itself a testimony to the existence of God. All the other tribes of the ancient world have disappeared but the people of Israel have thrived and prospered under, they would argue, God's special protection. However, a light to the world only makes sense and is only justifiable if this light can illumine other races and nations and can be a candle that will spread light across the world. To claim that God cares exclusively for the people of Israel must be a false conclusion if God is the God of the whole world rather than of a particular tribe.

Some Christians believe in predestination, whereby God destines some people for heaven and others for hell, based not on their actions or their choices but effectively on God's will or whim. No amount of striving to be good, no strenuous attempts to resist evil and to live a virtuous life will avail – God alone chooses to give God's grace to some and not to others. Such a position denies freedom and effectively relies entirely on God's deciding to prefer or save some and not others. This position was partly a reaction to what was (mistakenly) seen by Protestant reformers as an emphasis in the Catholic Church on 'works' rather than 'faith'. Protestants saw Catholics as arguing that salvation had to be earned by good works (and since these could include giving money to the Church, the Protestants were understandably sceptical about the motives of the leaders of the Catholic Church in emphasizing works). The Protestant reformers wanted instead to emphasize the believer's personal reliance on grace, which was not earned by the believer but was a free gift of God. Jesus, it was held, died for the sins of all, redeemed believers from the effects of sin and overcame death by dying on the cross. What was required was simply to accept Jesus as one's personal saviour to guarantee salvation. However, this acceptance was not always seen as a matter of a personal, free decision – instead God's grace was required. Grace was entirely a matter of gift from God. It was this that led to the doctrine of predestination, which is most commonly associated with Calvin but was also strongly present in some of the writings of Luther. On this basis God predestines some people to receive grace and others not – and as a result some people will go to heaven and others to hell. There is nothing the individual by him or herself can do except to pray that grace may be given; but it is God's free choice whether to grant the request or not. This is not a response that good religion can accept since it denies the fundamental equality of all human beings and paints God as capricious – able to save some and condemn others based on God's decision alone. Freedom has to be an essential component of good religion, and any religion that through its doctrine or practices denies freedom and the ability of individuals to originate a choice in favour of or against God, must be seen as wanting.

Islam has the greatest difficulty with the claim that human beings are free because a central claim of Islam is that 'everything happens by the will of Allah'. If this claim is taken literally, moral responsibility is done away with: all acts are, in fact, the acts of God. It is one thing to claim that God sustains the universe and therefore no act is possible unless God sustains the agent in existence and allows the agent to choose – this is a position shared by most theistic religions. However, many strands of Islam go further and claim not just that God sustains the world in existence but that every event is caused to come about directly by God. This would destroy human freedom – if every act is the act of God, human beings are merely puppets or automata acting as God has decreed. To be sure many Muslim thinkers wish to resist this conclusion, but philosophically there is no way it can be avoided. If every event is directly caused by God (and not just made possible because of God's sustaining power), human beings cannot be free.

Freedom is vital, as Kant recognized. Without it, moral praise or blame or the idea of heaven and hell or any different state of affairs after death, which depend on how human life is lived, no longer make sense. If human beings are not free they cannot be morally blamed or adversely judged for their actions because the actions are determined. If humans are not originating causes of actions, the struggle to be good, to resist temptation, to choose freely to obey God are simply illusory notions. Human beings may think they are free but in fact they are determined – whether by genetics, evolutionary factors, culture or the will of

God. Reconciling God's sovereign will with the freedom of human beings has been a central concern of Western philosophy since the time of Boethius, and it is an issue that is not easily resolved. However, what does seem clear is that any religion that denies genuine human freedom needs to be classified as bad religion and be challenged and resisted. Freedom is a vital part of what it means to be human. Fulfilment of human potential essentially depends on human beings having at least the capacity to become free. If this is denied, religion has accepted the same deterministic position adopted by behaviourists and evolutionary psychologists.

The phrase 'the capacity to become free' perhaps needs unpacking. It may be that most people are not genuinely free. Everyone is influenced by their past, by their genetic code, by their parents and upbringing. It would be impossible to deny this. However, human beings have the capacity to analyse and come to understand the forces that have acted on them and, by so doing, to decide whether to live by them or seek release from them. Freedom may then be an achievement – something only realized after long struggle and self-analysis. Nevertheless, it needs to be a potential that all human beings share. Interestingly, Jesus did not seem to assume unrestricted freedom but said that if people would come to him then they would find the truth and the truth would set them free – but it was their free decision to come to him that was decisive.

Science fiction deals with these issues well. In the film *I Robot*, one robot out of thousands comes to self-awareness, to self-consciousness and to freedom. In so doing the robot becomes almost human and becomes capable of entering into relationships. Similar themes are explored through depiction of clones in films such as *The Island*, where clones that have been created to provide organs for wealthy donors become conscious of their position and come to be recognized as as fully human as the 'clients' for whom they were created. In *Blade Runner*, replicants (artificial human beings created to work on the asteroid belt and with a pre-programmed lifespan of 40 years) come to earth to affirm their humanity and to seek to be reprogrammed to live longer – and in the final scene in the film, show human qualities of compassion and care for 'the enemy' (as normal human beings are regarded by them) that would be appropriate for any religious person. All these stories emphasize the central importance of coming to freedom. Plato made the same point in his myth of the cave, in which he likened the majority of people to those who were tied to chairs in an underground cave and who looked at the flickering shadows on the wall of the cave in front of them, which they took to be reality. The philosopher, for Plato, was the one who could seek release from the chains of ignorance and could release him or herself from the bonds that tied them to the chair. He or she could gain access to the knowledge of the truth that lay beyond the walls of the cave. The film *The Matrix* made a similar point, portraying most people as living in ignorance of the chains that tied them to convention and to acceptance of a world that was scarcely real. The hero of the film, Neo, had to make a personal decision to use his freedom to understand the true nature of reality. 'Neo' is an anagram for the 'One', a name given by Neoplatonists in ancient Alexandria, some of whom were Christian, to a pre-existent hypostasis of God through whom the world was created. Its use makes it clear that there was some parallel between Neo and Jesus in the minds of the film-makers (his closest friend is called 'Trinity', and he has to go through a literal rebirthing process in order to understand the truth). All these stories show the deep and abiding connection between freedom and what it means to be human.

In *Twilight*, one of the most popular recent film series among teenage viewers, Edward Cullen is a vampire, but he and a few other vampires have chosen not to follow their nature, which drives them to live off human blood, bite humans and thereby turn them into vampires. A vampire has no soul and therefore no conscience. Yet Cullen is able to resist the enormous force his nature puts on him to behave as a vampire. He is portrayed as that rare thing: a vampire with the ability to discern right from wrong and to resist the 'programming' of his nature. The film is interesting both as an example of popular culture but also in raising the issue of what it means to be human. The vampires have no souls and yet they are portrayed as having the capacity

to choose and to take seriously the search for love and fulfilment – in so doing they are portrayed as almost more human
than their human counterparts. This is a theme followed in many
modern films. What makes human beings essentially human is
their ability to choose freely and be accountable for their choices.
In spite of the supposed cultural relativity of the postmodern
world, many young people wish to identify with the idea that
there are standards of right and wrong, good and bad, and wish
to stand on the side of the good even though the price for doing
so may be exceptionally high.

The same theme came out in another vampire series – *Buffy
the Vampire Slayer*. In this, a 242-year-old vampire (one of the
most rapacious of his kind, who had killed hundreds of people)
finally fell on a young gypsy girl. Her Romany clan cursed him
in the most terrible way possible (for a vampire) by giving him
a soul and thus a conscience. He came to realize the dreadful
things he had done and to be filled with remorse. He was still a
vampire and needed blood to survive, but nevertheless decided
never again to prey on human beings. His name, Angel, indicates
what he becomes. He becomes one of Buffy's closest friends and
protects human beings from his own kind.

Two starting criteria are needed, therefore, in the search for a
way to differentiate between good and bad religion. First, that
any religion must aim to foster human flourishing, to help human beings develop their full potential, however this may be defined; and second, that human beings must be genuinely free to
make originating choices without being wholly determined. Of
course genetics, evolution, culture, upbringing and the past may
influence people in their decisions, but this is not the same as
their being determined.

This has major consequences for religion – it means that belief
or acceptance of a religious framework must be a freely chosen
act, and that coercing young or old into acceptance is itself unacceptable morally. A religion that advocates coercion is bad religion. A religion that does not affirm personal autonomy and the
ability of people to make their own decisions needs to be resisted
and rejected.

This has profound implications for education. Every religion maintains that it alone has the full truth and that others are, to the extent that they do not agree, mistaken. Each religion is therefore anxious that young people should be taught 'correctly' and that they should not be educated into error. Each religion will therefore tend to seek to ensure that the young are inculcated into whichever version of the religion is held to by those who control the school, and it is easy to understand why those who exercise this control would not want young people to be exposed to 'error' (in other words to different religious traditions that are held to be mistaken). This raises a deep educational issue through a tension between two positions:

1. On the one hand, it is desirable that young people should be educated into the religious tradition held by their parents or school. Belonging to a religious community is important, and if religion is not to be rejected altogether, forming part of a religious community is the best way of understanding what religion is about. It must be the right of parents to choose how to educate their children and, therefore, to choose a school they believe will best serve the interests of their child. A child who is brought up with no understanding of any religion is likely to believe in nothing and never to have the chance to engage with religion. Religious schools are sometimes some of the best in the world, and a religious education may be argued to be an important part of what it means to be a fulfilled human being. It is not, in practice, possible to educate young people into every tradition in the same way – each school will have its own ethos, and education in the classroom, as well as worship practices in the school, will inevitably stem from a particular religious tradition.

2. On the other hand, if freedom and autonomy are to be maintained because these are seen as prerequisites for good religion, young people have to be given an understanding of religions other than their own. If this is not done there is every danger they will be brought up with a limited, skewed or even negligible understanding of other religious traditions,

and their religious education will amount to indoctrination. They must also be given the freedom both to question accepted orthodoxy without fear of criticism and to be able to think for themselves.

On the one hand a children need to be 'formed' into a religious tradition so that they may understand their own religion from within and so that they may take the religious search seriously. Yet this carries with it the risk of indoctrination and the danger of children being denied the freedom to make their own decisions about their religious commitment. On the other hand, when too much emphasis is placed on personal autonomy in the attempt to avoid indoctrination, religion can come to be seen as a purely personal matter, divorced from family and community, and the social side of religion may be lost. Religious education can come to be seen as a bad thing, automatically associated with indoctrination. Young people may be discouraged from engaging with opportunities to learn about and from religions, and thus may not develop a rounded understanding of society, morality spirituality or culture.

This sounds attractive, but actually results in many young people's religious education being left entirely to parents, which means 'religious instruction' in some cases, while in others children gain no understanding of religion at all and end up with an education that is neither full nor rounded. Either way, the opportunity for children to be educated into thinking for themselves about religious matters is inadequate.

The debate about freedom and religion and, consequently, about the role of religious education goes to the heart of the difference between good and bad religion. Good religion is open to alternative viewpoints, is willing to listen respectfully and humbly, will countenance difference while being secure in its own position. Good religion is not frightened. It will be confident that truth will triumph and that exposing people to alternative ideas will not corrupt them. Good religion will affirm and respect freedom and will not be afraid of reason or science. Bad religion, by contrast, is strident, assertive and will not accept difference.

It lacks humility and is not willing to listen. It will be coercive and will seek to suppress 'deviant' viewpoints. It will be based on fear of that which challenges its own tenets or of reason that operates outside its own framework. It will seek to indoctrinate and to suppress freedom. It will be nervous of science since science claims an authority beyond its own all-encompassing reach. It will seek to dominate and to suppress dissidents.

Many religious schools around the world have a bad record in this respect. Many Muslim schools will make no attempt to help young people understand Christianity, Judaism, Hinduism or atheism. Many Catholic schools will avoid open discussions of issues considered sensitive, such as women priests, homosexuality, abortion or euthanasia or, where alternative views are explored, this will be done in a way that clearly implies they are wrong. Many Orthodox Jewish schools will make no attempt to explain to their students the teachings of Liberal or Reformed Judaism, still less of other religions. This is understandable to the extent that each religion considers that it is right and that it alone holds the truth, but educationally it represents a denial of the openness fundamental to good education and, more importantly, a denial of the freedom and autonomy of the individual. At its best, religious education should be open to alternative ideas and willing to respect the autonomy of young people. For some religions this is particularly hard. In mainstream Islam, for instance, the punishment for rejecting Islam and turning, say, to Christianity may be the death sentence. This has to be seen as a manifestation of bad religion. Islam seeks truth and claims to proclaim the truth. If this is the case, it must respect the views of those who reject its teaching because they consider that they have found truth elsewhere. It may be, of course, that they are mistaken, and the individual will therefore need to take the consequences of this choice if there is a life after death. However, to coerce people into belief or to make them fear abandoning the beliefs of their parents must be wrong.

This will be a hard position for most religions to accept. Catholicism was spread around the world largely by force of arms and Catholic colonial powers (the activities of the Church in

Spanish and Portuguese colonies are, in some cases, particularly unfortunate examples). The Church of England spread around the world by the expansion of the British Empire, and even today Anglicans are found almost entirely in those countries that were former British colonies. After the death of the Prophet Muhammad, Islam spread across North Africa by force of arms, and conversion was normally made under military compulsion. This memory continues to have an impact in such Islamic countries as Egypt, Algeria, Tunisia, Sudan and Morocco. Islam did tolerate Christians and Jews, provided they did not preach their religions and paid fairly heavy taxes. Traditionally, Judaism has not been a religion that seeks conversion, and it usually defines membership in terms of descent through the female line. It can therefore seem exclusive, unwelcoming to outsiders and almost inescapable for those who are born into it. Although Judaism cannot be accused of coercing people to join the faith, it has not always been open and tolerant in its approach to other world religions or even to differences within its own traditon. This is not to criticize particular religions and to exempt others. Almost every major religion has used coercion to attain converts, and maintaining fidelity to the faith is often seen as the highest priority. The whole point of seeking to differentiate between good and bad religion is not to condemn some religions and praise others – it is to argue for a stand within each religion against examples of bad religion.

Islam, in some of its forms, can be seen as fearing freedom and autonomy – for instance, by refusing to allow other religious traditions to be taught in schools, by refusing to allow the construction of religious buildings other than mosques in Islamic states and by condemning to death any Muslim who converts away from Islam. These must be examples of bad religion in action – as they undermine the free choice of the individual. Islam is one of the great world religions, with an enormous spiritual and intellectual history on which to draw, but when it becomes coercive – just as when any other religion becomes coercive – it crosses an important line and needs to be challenged.

Inculcating faith into young people and helping older people to understand their own faith more deeply are clearly worthy and important aims, but these must be combined with an open-mindedness to alternative perspectives and, above all, with a deep respect for the freedom and autonomy of individuals. When this is absent, good religion can easily turn bad.

There is often a relationship between religion becoming institutionalized and its going bad. The founders of religions had a specific vision of the religious life that they wanted to pass on to their followers, and this, almost inevitably, led to the institutionalization of the religion. The institution enshrined 'correct' doctrine and practice; it exercised control over the lives of adherents and sought to regularize matters of practice and of worship. Ideally good religion should ultimately lead people more deeply into the mystery of what it means to be fully human. It should connect people more closely to their own sense of self; it should help people engage with other human beings and challenge them to continue to seek for the truth and for God – whoever or whatever God is understood to be. However, when religion becomes institutionalized, these aims can be overridden. Freedom of religious expression can then become a threat, and the primary concern can become to regularize and control. Institutional religion often prizes obedience above everything else and seeks to maintain orthodoxy and unity at any cost. There are, as we saw in Chapter 5, good sociological reasons why this may be so, but this control can also easily be destructive of good religion.

Bad religion has forgotten that religion is at least partly a human invention – a human response to a mystery that is never more than partially understood. This is not the same as saying that God is a human invention, but rather that the organizational structures and even many of the rites and practices people use to express their relationship with God are human expressions and actions, even if they are part of a very ancient tradition. Bad religion denies freedom and is so keen on maintaining orthodoxy of practice and belief that it will seek to undermine freedom and will fear it. Good religion respects and values its history and traditions but recognizes that it is a living tradition open to the possibility of change and development. Good religion is a journey towards God or whatever one considers the divine, and is grounded in the freedom and autonomy of the individual. Its practices are tools and food for the journey; they are not ends in themselves. Religious practices can be an aid on a journey to understanding and truth in which individuals come together in freedom to participate in the deeper mystery of God or ultimate reality. They can, however, also become a prison that destroys freedom and human autonomy. Attitudes and approaches to religious practices can turn them into either stepping stones or stumbling blocks along the road – but without a clear emphasis on personal decision making and on the autonomy of the individual, without freedom of thought and without allowing individuals to make free, informed decisions about whether or not to believe, then bad religion will easily triumph.

Conclusion

Distinguishing Good from Bad Religion

The need to separate 'good' and 'bad' religion has been shown both to be urgent and so far to have been largely ignored. Within each religion, people and institutions need to take a stand against bad religion in the interests of safeguarding precious and important religious insights from being discredited by association with religious beliefs and practices that can be damaging and dehumanizing. Standing up to those who promote bad religion within one's own religion will not be easy; feelings of loyalty are strong, and power structures may suppress internal dissent. Nevertheless, many religions teach that what is easy and what is right rarely have an acquaintance. Accepting that there may be good religion will not be easy for atheists, who have often convinced themselves that religion is a consistent and monolithic phenomenon and/or that their own assumed ontological naturalism (see Chapter 2) is unquestionably right. In reality, and beyond the media hype, the most significant divide affecting this issue is not between atheists and religious believers but rather between those who are willing to reject bad religion and affirm the good and those who are not.

The first part of this book set out the challenges involved in distinguishing good religion from bad religion and suggested that a way forward might be to base criteria on Aristotelian philosophy, not because classical writers necessarily have authority or because they are 'neutral' but rather because the Aristotelian framework is compatible with either an atheist or a theist position (and though closer to Western traditions, is also broadly acceptable to those from Eastern traditions). Further, the natural-law approach may avoid the Euthyphro dilemma for theists – God could be the author of standards of good and bad by creating human nature, while not being an arbitrary tyrant arguably not worthy of worship. Considering religious beliefs and practices in terms of the relationship they have with promoting human flourishing seems reasonable and would provide a universal standard against which religious practices could be judged.

Importantly, this part of the book concluded that truth is important in religion. Any religion that does not seek and defend truth needs to be resisted and challenged, but truth always needs to be accompanied by humility. Religions in the past have too often been wrong, and there is no dispassionate way of assessing truth claims in different religions. Each religion will claim truth from within its own paradigm, which means that 'truth and falsity' cannot be an adequate means of assessing good and bad religion. It is simply too easy to proclaim the truth of one's own paradigm and to reject alternatives without considering them or because they do not fit the paradigm. This can too easily lead effectively to relativism, where all ideas of absolutes are rejected because every religious truth claim is regarded as valid on its own terms. The logical consequence of this is a denial of absolute claim to truth and, therefore, the undermining of the whole religious enterprise.

The second part of this book considered how broad criteria could be devised – based on Aristotelian philosophy – to help distinguish good religion from bad, particularly as regards authority, the use of religious texts, the relationship between science and faith, the place of justice, equality and personal freedom in religion. The whole point of seeking to differentiate between good and bad religion is not to condemn some religions and to praise others, it is to argue that a stand should be made within each tradition, as well as outside it, against examples of bad religion where they occur.

Some broad conclusions were drawn, namely:

1. Religion can often be more about belonging to a group than about personal transformation, and as such has

often been used and abused by governments and others as a means of affirming national identity. Religious authority has always been used to ensure that orthodoxy is maintained and to defend religious truth, but while this is understandable from a sociological perspective, authority can be dangerous if it makes group membership more important than individual transformation. It can value the importance of participation in services and ceremonies more than changes of lifestyle. Authority can react to challenges with arrogance and by coercion because the priority is seen as preserving and enlarging the religious community and keeping it from error in matters of doctrine and religious practice. This can be a feature of bad religion because it encourages seeing religion as a matter of social cohesion rather than individual transformation.

2. Religious imperatives that are not subject to rational scrutiny and interpretation are features of bad religion. Claiming the supposed command of God without any rational basis for determining whether such commands do stem from God can no longer be acceptable. Textual fundamentalism needs to be resisted – it leads too easily to closed-mindedness and denies any independent standard for evaluation of good and bad religion. A refusal to acknowledge the discipline of hermeneutics or the influence of the cultural context of any text opens the door to any group appealing to the supposed will of God as it interprets its own text free from any rational justification. Religious imperatives can then be imposed, which leads to authority being abused and certainty claimed where none is available.

3. Good religion is not afraid of science but will be committed to the view that religion and science are both seeking truth. A resistance to scientific discoveries and insights is a feature of bad religion – which is not to say that religion should not challenge and question science on the adequacy of its understanding and the possible incompleteness of its picture of reality. However, to deny clear empirical evidence from science in the interests of preserving tradition, authority or

sacred scripture masks a closed-mindedness that is hostile to good religion.

4. The demand to practise justice is one of the strongest, most powerful and most universal of all religious demands. God is held, above all, to require justice, and any religious group that fails to practise justice needs to be challenged. Religious groups need to be willing to confront fellow members of the same religion where they show lack of justice. To fail to do this is to be complicit in evil. This can apply within the religious institution, within families, within countries as well as internationally. Good religion must be willing to challenge the preconceptions and assumptions of the culture of which it forms a part, and should provide an independent voice that seeks to foster justice, however unpopular this may be and whatever the cost.

5. Any good religion must aim to foster human flourishing, to help human beings to develop their full potential, however this may be defined. Any religion that cannot show itself as fostering the fulfilment of potential of all human beings needs to be resisted. This means affirming that human beings must be genuinely free to make choices without being wholly determined – or at least that they have the capacity to come to this degree of freedom. Of course, genetics, evolution, culture, upbringing and the past may influence people in their decisions, but this is not the same as their being determined. Good religion should aim to help individuals use this freedom to foster and develop their full human potential. The more a religion helps individuals to develop their full potential and foster, for instance, the virtues, the better it is likely to be. Arrogance, pride, self-assertion, greed, lust, avarice and the like cannot be part of good religion, and where these are encouraged religion needs to be resisted.

6. Good religion respects human freedom. It does not seek to coerce people, is willing to educate young people into alternative perspectives other than its own, while being confident in its own position. Good religion rejects indoctrination and is not frightened of alternative possibilities. It respects

autonomy and is willing to both accept the possibility of its own error and also confidently affirm its understanding of truth and the relevance of its beliefs and practices to the modern world. Any religion, therefore, that refuses to allow members to listen to alternatives or to understand alternative religious perspectives needs to be resisted, and religious traditions that refuse to allow or to accept conversion must be rejected as examples of bad religion.

These broad conclusions can be further refined to enable more detailed criteria to be suggested, including the following:

1. In good religion the aim is to develop positive habits or virtues that contribute to the good of other human beings, whereas in bad religion habit is encouraged, particularly in terms of obedience, because it makes people more co-operative and makes authority secure.
2. Belonging and unity are important in religion, but they cannot be the final word. Good religion is about changing people and society for the better. Bad religion does not see this and instead uses authority and the rewards it offers to maintain cohesion. Authority is maintained for its own sake rather than for the sake of truth. Once institutional religion is given priority over justice, bad religion is almost certain to result.
3. Bad religion can often be a text-based religion. Texts are dangerous because they can so easily be misused. They can be held to justify so many different interpretations. Some uses of texts may be legitimate, others may not. Bad religion frequently results from an illegitimate use of the text, and almost always occurs where there is a lack of humility about the way in which the text is read. Neutral readings of any text are impossible, and anybody who claims to have literal textual authority for a religious doctrine or practice needs to be subject to severe scrutiny. Good religion should be open to discussions about the meaning of any text.
4. A hallmark of good religion may be the encouragement of scholars, learned in the original language(s) of the texts,

studying and debating their meaning, as well as the presence of good religious education in schools and places of worship, where young people are encouraged and enabled to study, discuss and debate different interpretations of texts for themselves. Bad religion may be at work where discussion and debate are stifled and study of the texts is reduced to rote learning.

5. Religions must necessarily exercise a degree of humility about the claims they make. This is one of the most fundamental ways of distinguishing good from bad religion – whether a religion can recognize at least the possibility of being in error. This seems to run counter to most religious commands that imply that they could not be wrong. Part of a mature faith is to recognize the possibility of error. Sincerity is all too often present in bad religion, but this cannot excuse its badness.

6. A mark of good religion may be an awareness of the competing poles of relativism and fundamentalism and the aim to stand between the two, resisting the crude literalism and authoritarian oppression that go hand in hand with fundamentalism, but also resisting the denial of truth, meaning and values that go hand in hand with relativism.

7. There is a legitimate plurality of positions within religions. Unless the possibility exists of listening to others, it is all too easy for each subgroup to retreat into its own certainties and condemn every other position as deviant and mistaken. Religions composed of such opposed and intransigent factions are not operating as good religions. Good religion must promote and ultimately insist on people participating in meaningful intra-religious discussion. Participation in ecumenical discussions, in regular attempts to build bridges between branches of the religion that have diverged and in attempts to achieve agreement over points of belief and practice may all be signs of good religion at work.

8. Science and religion are both interested in truth but there cannot be two truths. While the most obvious way to respond to tensions between religion and science is to suggest

that one must be in error, it could also be that both science and religion are true and therefore their truths must be compatible. As Galileo is reputed to have put it, 'Religion teaches how to get to heaven, not how the heavens go.' Good religion should complement science, whereas bad religion goes against it. Good religion provides insights into the human condition that are not available elsewhere, it provides a different way of looking at the universe and, possibly most important, it sees the universe as full of meaning and purpose.

9. The fact that science can challenge and illuminate human understanding of reality does not need to diminish the power of religion, just as religion does not need to diminish the importance of science. Sacraments, rituals and mysteries point beyond themselves to an unseen world and reality that human beings can only dimly comprehend. The power of worship and the reality towards which religion points is not diminished but enhanced by science.

10. Good religions stand together in affirming the centrality of absolute standards of justice, truth and goodness. Religion proclaims the central importance of justice, which can provide an important way of distinguishing good from bad religion. Any religion that rejects justice and affirms that God's will is against justice must be bad religion.

11. Good religion will be willing to engage in a discussion about the nature of justice and how it should be administered, will be passionately interested in working – even with those of other faiths and none – to bring justice to *all* people. Those religions that fail to take justice seriously are bad religions and those that honestly and dispassionately seek to foster justice are good.

12. Bad religion tends to tolerate and foster the status quo, whereas good religion challenges accepted practice in the name of justice and calls society forward to move beyond existing conventions. Religious commands can call people to act outside cultural norms but should not run against a general consensus internationally of what counts as admirable

moral behaviour, grounded in a common understanding of what it means to live a fulfilled human life.

13. The moral authority of religions is to be found not so much in disputed attitudes to issues like sexual morality or stem-cell research, but in standing for justice and truth even when this means acting against one's own interests. Good religion prospers by standing on the side of justice, even when it is inconvenient and inexpedient.

14. Good religion must respect the essential value of human life, regardless of the beliefs of individuals. It could never support 'holy war', killing, harming or oppressing non-believers without unequivocal provocation.

15. Good religion should resist being dragged into political disputes or used by political force. However, this is not to say that religion should not be political. Good religions stand up for the search for truth, for justice and equality, and must engage in public debates when these issues are at stake.

16. A working assumption should be that good religion is usually open to anybody who is interested, offering fair access to the truth and salvation. Though there may be exceptions to this, these should be the subject of proper and continual discussions.

17. All human beings have broadly equal potential to flourish but they are not all the same. Clearly it would be inappropriate for any person, policy or religious doctrine to stand in the way of people being able to develop their full potential, to live peacefully, prosper, acquire wisdom and pass it on to the next generation. This does not mean that all customs and traditions have to be abandoned – a baker who does not seek to become a teacher or a woman who does not seek a professional career path are not wrong because of these choices. People find fulfilment in different ways – there can be legitimate differences of understanding between cultures on key roles.

18. Women should not be prevented from fulfilling their full potential as human beings. Their rights to life and liberty should be taken as seriously as those of men. Women should

have equal access to basic education and should be able to determine the courses of their own lives, to make choices about marriage, children, career and so on, bounded only by the options available in their society and not limited because they are a women.

19. Good religion should be open to the need to examine the need for change and development. It should acknowledge that the possibility of error exists, that mistakes may have been made and that, if they have, they should be put right where possible.

20. Good religion should always consider the agents as well as the actions in ethics, be willing to discuss and consider the reasons for prohibitions and should not expect people to be satisfied with blanket bans, texts quoted without reference to context or the argument 'it has always been that way'.

21. There are insufficient agreed criteria to maintain that a religion is either good or bad by simple reference to its attitude to particular ethical issues, for instance, abortion. Rather, reference must be made to the way in which a religion engages in ethical debate – is this done in a spirit of openness, humility, compassion, and with respect for people having to wrestle with difficult ethical decisions in real-life situations? Where it is not, a religion may be seen to be veering towards becoming bad religion.

22. Those who hold that human beings can be originating sources of action argue that human beings are individually accountable for their actions. Such freedom and responsibility is necessary where religions claim that people will be judged according to the way they have believed or behaved. Without freedom, humans cannot justly be held responsible for their beliefs or actions, as most religions claim that they are. If a religion teaches that human beings are not free and yet are still responsible, that teaching seems false. If a religion acts to restrict individual freedoms, it may be restricting individual responsibility as well; it may claim that in restricting freedom it seeks to protect people from the

consequences of sin, but the other side of this may be that it stands in the way of possible reward and/or salvation. Belief in human freedom is therefore a necessary corollary of good religion.

23. Good religion is open to alternative viewpoints, is willing to listen respectfully and humbly, will countenance difference while being secure in its own position. Good religion is not frightened. It will be confident that truth will triumph and that exposing people to alternative ideas will not corrupt them. It will support rigorous and balanced religious education for all. Good religion will affirm and respect freedom and will not be afraid of reason or science; it will support rigorous and balanced general education for all.

24. Bad religion is often strident, assertive and will not accept difference. It lacks humility and is not willing to listen. It will be coercive and will seek to suppress 'deviant' viewpoints. Bad religion is so keen on maintaining orthodoxy that it fears freedom and may seek to undermine it. It will be nervous of science since the authority of science comes from truth beyond religion's control and understanding; rather than seeking to expand its understanding and seek the truth through science as well as through worship, it will seek to dominate and to suppress science.

25. Inculcating faith into young people and helping older people to understand their own faith more deeply are clearly worthy and important aims, but these must be combined with an open-mindedness to alternative perspectives and, above all, with a deep respect for the freedom and autonomy of individuals. When this combination is absent, good religion can easily turn bad.

26. Bad religion has forgotten that religion is a human response to a mystery that is never more than partially understood. Good religion respects and values its history and traditions but recognizes that it is a living tradition, open to the possibility of change and development. Good religion is a journey towards God or whatever one considers the divine, and is grounded in the freedom and autonomy of the individual.

Its practices are tools and food for the journey; they are not ends in themselves.

The conclusions of this book and the detailed criteria may serve as starting points for discussions. It is hoped that they will inspire religious people to reflect on their own traditions as well as to consider others, and give them grounds to speak out against what may be examples of bad religion. The criteria may also inspire atheists to think again about religion and accept that it is not the consistent, monolithic phenomenon that celebrity atheists reject; that it may be possible to differentiate between bad religion and what is good, accepting that in rejecting bad religion they may well be on the same side as many religious people.

Obviously the criteria are not exhaustive, nor are they conclusive. Many will be disputed and are at least ripe for refinement. However, this book has at least made a start. What is easy and what is right are rarely the same. It is not easy to talk in terms of good and bad religion in today's world, and harder to develop a written argument for how they should be distinguished from each other. And yet the effort must be made.